TEBOW
TIME

TEBOW
TIME

Insights on Winning from
Football's Rising Star

by Jesse Hines

JEREMY P. TARCHER/PENGUIN
a member of Penguin Group (USA) Inc.
New York

JEREMY P. TARCHER/PENGUIN
Published by the Penguin Group
Penguin Group (USA) Inc., 375 Hudson Street, New York, New York 10014, USA •
Penguin Group (Canada), 90 Eglinton Avenue East, Suite 700, Toronto, Ontario
M4P 2Y3, Canada (a division of Pearson Penguin Canada Inc.) • Penguin Books
Ltd, 80 Strand, London WC2R 0RL, England • Penguin Ireland, 25 St Stephen's
Green, Dublin 2, Ireland (a division of Penguin Books Ltd) • Penguin Group
(Australia), 250 Camberwell Road, Camberwell, Victoria 3124, Australia
(a division of Pearson Australia Group Pty Ltd) • Penguin Books India Pvt Ltd,
11 Community Centre, Panchsheel Park, New Delhi–110 017, India • Penguin
Group (NZ), 67 Apollo Drive, Rosedale, North Shore 0632, New Zealand
(a division of Pearson New Zealand Ltd) • Penguin Books (South Africa)
(Pty) Ltd, 24 Sturdee Avenue, Rosebank, Johannesburg 2196, South Africa

Penguin Books Ltd, Registered Offices: 80 Strand, London WC2R 0RL, England

All Scriptures herein are taken from the New American Standard Bible,
unless otherwise noted.

Most Tarcher/Penguin books are available at special quantity discounts
for bulk purchase for sales promotions, premiums, fund-raising, and educational
needs. Special books or book excerpts also can be created to fit specific needs.
For details, write Penguin Group (USA) Inc. Special Markets,
375 Hudson Street, New York, NY 10014.

ISBN 978-0-399-16232-9

Printed in the United States of America
1   3   5   7   9   10   8   6   4   2

BOOK DESIGN BY AMANDA DEWEY

For my parents,

Robert and Lucy Hines,

who instilled in me a passion
for reading and writing

CONTENTS

My greatest goal in my life is that when I'm in heaven and I'm standing before Jesus Christ, He opens up His arms, and He walks up to me, and He gives me a hug, and He says, "Timmy, great job. You finished. That-a-boy."

—*"Roy L. White Legacy Golf and Gala,"*
Union University, April 19, 2010

AUTHOR'S NOTE

The book in your hands will grant you a deeper insight into who Tim Tebow is, and what drives him to excel, both on the football field and in life. The one hundred quotations contained in this book present Tebow's thoughts on his approach to winning in all of life—covering his football career, his faith, his upbringing, how he deals with both adoration and criticism, his obsession with hard work, his passion for improving the lives of others, and many other topics.

The quotes are culled from interviews, press conferences, profile pieces, speeches, and other public statements Tebow has given throughout his career—from high school, college, and the NFL.

Each quote is followed by a few paragraphs of commentary by the editor, setting Tebow's words in their proper context. The commentaries explain the circumstances surrounding Tebow's remarks, give examples of how the ideas expressed in the quotes manifest themselves in his life, and connect Tebow's insights to the theme of winning.

Tebow is passionately committed to winning, and to

working harder than anyone else in that pursuit—coaches and reporters note that he is the first on the practice field and the last off it. He tries to outrun everyone else in wind sprints during practice, his teammates say. But he is even more passionate about his relationship with Jesus Christ, which for him means living each day to the glory of God and using his influence to bring a brighter day, both physically and emotionally, to suffering people.

He has said many times that positively affecting the lives of others is far more meaningful to him than football success. For Tebow, a true winning life is not possible without faith in Jesus Christ and, while he doggedly pursues temporal, earthly prizes, his ultimate goal in life is to win eternal rewards in heaven.

Whether Tim Tebow becomes one of the NFL's great players or washes out in a few years, he will remain a force in American culture for years to come. His charitable foundation work will continue. And he has already said that he thinks and prays about running for political office.

This book contains motivational quotes from Tebow that will encourage readers to work hard in the pursuit of their own goals, to tune out their naysayers without getting vindictive, to boldly, yet gently, proclaim their faith even when it's not popular, to help the suffering and needy, and above all, to treasure their faith with Jesus Christ as the supreme joy in life and to live to the glory of God.

INTRODUCTION

A man will be satisfied with good
by the fruit of his words,
And the deeds of a man's hands
will return to him.

PROVERBS 12:14

Why publish a book of quotes from a young NFL quarterback?

Fair question.

The answer: His name is Tim Tebow.

In case you're one of the few who are unfamiliar with Tebow, here's a snapshot of his fame:

- Tebow was voted America's most popular active professional athlete by sports fans, according to the ESPN Sports Poll conducted in December 2011.
- Tebow's autobiography, *Through My Eyes*, released when he was twenty-three, was a *New York Times* bestseller.

- Tebow was named to the 2012 *Time* magazine 100 Most Influential People in the World list.
- Tebow spoke at an outdoor Easter service in 2012 that drew 15,000 people.
- *Saturday Night Live* devoted a skit to Tebow, and he has appeared on *Jimmy Kimmel Live!*, *Late Night with Jimmy Fallon*, *The Daily Show*, and numerous sports and news programs.
- President Barack Obama praised Tebow as a role model for America's youth, and Republican presidential candidates sought his endorsement.

It's true that Tebow's professional football career is in its early stages (he spent his first two years with the Denver Broncos before joining the New York Jets), but it's also true that he is America's most popular and most controversial athlete. He generates enormous media coverage whenever he plays a game, holds a press conference, speaks at a church, or simply has dinner with a female. It seems that whatever he does, no matter how noteworthy or not worthy of attention, it is nevertheless reported on and endlessly discussed.

In fact, Tebow's prominence and influence transcends the sports world, spilling over into the realms of religion, social issues, politics, entertainment, and humanitarianism. Clearly, there is something unique about this young man that resonates with so many people. Tebow's standout attributes combined with his background and accomplishments make his thoughts on winning worthy of consideration.

A WINSOME WINNER

Tebow receives so much attention, firstly, because he has been a winner wherever he goes.

Winning: He played for two high school football state championship teams and two college football championship teams, setting many quarterback records in both leagues. He won his state's award for high school football player of the year twice and he won the Heisman Trophy for best college football player. In 2011, his first full year as an NFL starting quarterback, after taking over when the Denver Broncos were 1–4 and in last place in their division, Tebow led them to an 8–8 record, a first place finish in their division, and into the playoffs. Tebow then engineered an overtime playoff victory against the league's number-one-rated defense, the Pittsburgh Steelers.

But if Tebow just won football games, he would simply be another highly popular athlete instead of the cultural icon that he has become. Part of what makes him such a compelling figure is his open and enthusiastic expression of his Christian faith, his humble demeanor, and his deep commitment to charity work.

Christianity: "First and foremost, I just want to thank my Lord and Savior, Jesus Christ," is how Tebow often begins interviews and press conferences after games, ending them with "God bless." In college, he wrote Scriptures on his eye black (grease applied under the eyes to reduce sunlight glare) for games. After college, he appeared in a pro-life ad for Focus on the Family during the 2010 Super Bowl. The ad referenced his mother's refusal to abort him for religious reasons, despite her doctors' recommendation that she do so to protect her health.

Humility: Tebow rarely, if ever, brags about himself. Instead, he praises his teammates and coaches, and often his opponents, win or lose. He emits a warm smile, and speaks without condescension or conceit. When asked to respond to specific critics, he tends to first say something positive about them, and then addresses the criticism without saying anything vindictive about the critic in return.

Charity: Through his charity organization, the Tim Tebow Foundation, Tebow brings a sick child or adult and his or her family to each game he plays, whether at home or away, and visits with them before and after the game. His foundation supports an orphanage in the Philippines, where he has traveled several times to personally minister to the children. His foundation is also building playrooms in children's hospitals, as well as partnering with CURE International to construct children's hospitals in the developing world.

That mixture of winning, humility, and good works, however, still doesn't fully explain why people care about Tebow so much. Also relevant are his style of football play, his underdog status, and his penchant for engineering dramatic comeback victories.

Playing Style: Although he's a quarterback, Tebow often tucks the ball under his arm and runs, smashing headfirst into defenders to fight for extra yards. Unlike most quarterbacks who slide before contact with defenders, Tebow tries to run right through them. He has unleashed numerous highlight-worthy runs throughout his years in high school, college, and the NFL. He is also emotionally expressive on the field, throwing his hands up and yelling in joy after scores, as well as taking a knee for a quick prayer in the end zone ("Tebowing").

Underdog Status: From Pop Warner to high school to college—and now in the NFL—Tebow has endured constant criticism for his quarterbacking ability. When he was younger, coaches wanted to employ his large, muscular frame on defense as a linebacker. In college, critics said he was a "system quarterback" who could only play in offensive schemes designed around the shotgun and option formations. NFL draft experts said he could not play quarterback in the pros and would not be a first-round pick (he was). Now, even after taking the Denver Broncos to the playoffs in his first year as a starter and winning in the first round, many football observers continue to pan Tebow for his throwing motion, footwork, ability to read defenses, and passing accuracy, declaring that he will never be a successful starting quarterback in the NFL.

Comeback Wins: Throughout his breakout season with Denver, Tebow produced five comeback victories in the regular season, culminating with an overtime playoff victory, hence, the birth of the term "Tebow Time," designating the time when, late in the game with his team behind, Tebow steps in to pull out a close victory.

Finally, a look at Tebow's story and background more fully explains his popularity and why he has unique insights to offer when it comes to the concept of winning.

THE TIM TEBOW STORY IN BRIEF

Tim Tebow almost didn't make it into this world. His parents' doctors recommended they seek an abortion due to health complications arising during the pregnancy. His mother suffered a life-threatening infection, and several times the Tebows thought Tim had died before birth. Deeply religious—the Tebows were Christian missionaries to the Philippines at the time—an abortion was unthinkable. Believing all life is valuable and a gift from God, Bob and Pam Tebow decided to keep the baby and trust Him with the outcome.

On August 14, 1987, in Makati City, Philippines, Timothy Richard Tebow was born, the youngest of five Tebow children. He was skinny, but otherwise healthy, and grew to become strong and athletic, now standing six-foot-three and 245 pounds.

Three years later, in 1990, the Tebows moved back to Jacksonville, Florida. Tebow began playing sports at a young age, trying to be like his older brothers and competing with them. At the age of six, Tebow prayed to accept Jesus Christ into his heart as his Lord and Savior, which he says is the most important thing that has ever happened to him.

Tebow, like his two sisters and two brothers before him, was homeschooled from kindergarten through high school. School days often began with a reading of the Psalm of the day and the Proverb of the day. Though homeschooled, Tebow began his high school football career at Trinity Christian Academy of Jacksonville, a private school, playing quarterback as an eighth grader for the junior varsity team. He wanted to play quarterback for the varsity team the following year, but was told by the coaches that he was too big and athletic for that position. As a freshman, Tebow instead played linebacker and tight end. He helped Trinity win the Florida Class 4A state championship.

Not willing to give up on his dream of playing quarterback, Tebow and his father searched for a coach who was willing to play him at that position and was also a man they could trust and respect. The Tebows chose Craig Howard, head football coach at Allen D. Nease High School in Ponte Vedra Beach, Florida. Tebow and his mother moved into an apartment in the school's district to qualify him to play for Nease, a public school, where he transferred for his sophomore year.

Tebow began attracting national media attention in 2004, as a junior quarterback for the Nease Panthers. He was named Florida's Player of the Year, garnering attention as a major college recruit.

Because of his athletic success and his unique story—Tebow was putting up huge statistics and he once played an entire second half with a broken leg—ESPN aired a documentary in December 2005 that followed him through his senior year, called *Tim Tebow: The Chosen One*. As a senior, Tebow led the Nease Panthers to victory in the state championship. He repeated as Florida's High School Player of the Year, and was named Florida's Mr. Football. He was also chosen as a *Parade* magazine high school All-American.

According to the ESPN documentary, Tebow received eighty college football scholarship offers. He chose to attend the University of Florida and soon became one of college football's most celebrated players. He won the Heisman Trophy for the 2007 season, and helped Florida win the national championship in the 2006 and 2008 seasons. In 2009, *Sports Illustrated* named Tebow the College Football Player of the Decade.

A second documentary on Tebow, which followed him from his last college game to the 2010 NFL draft day, when the Denver Broncos selected him in the first round, aired on ESPN in January 2011. It was entitled *Tim Tebow: Everything in Between*.

The 2011 NFL season was when Tim Tebow became TIM TEBOW to the American public at large, as his magical season with the Denver Broncos took him from being a well-known football player to a cultural icon.

Action

It's not the dreamers that are remembered, it's the doers. Just having a dream doesn't mean much if you don't start at it. You have to take action. Every day I try to do something to get better.

—Big Atlantic Classic tip-off banquet, January 31, 2010

In Context

As a boy, Tebow dreamed of playing quarterback in the NFL. Despite leading his teams to championship victories, winning numerous awards, and setting statistical records as a quarterback for both Nease High School and the University of Florida, NFL draft experts roundly decried Tebow's quarterbacking ability. They said his defensive coverage reading, footwork, throwing motion, and passing accuracy were poor.

Despite that, Tebow's dream propelled his actions, and he put in constant practice to improve his weak areas in the months leading up to the draft. Many commentators admitted that by draft day, his throwing motion had noticeably improved. The hard work paid off, as Tebow was selected with the 25th pick in the first round by the Denver Broncos. In his second year with Denver, he became the starting quarterback, leading the Broncos to first place in their division and to an overtime victory in the first round of the playoffs.

Adaptability

There definitely are times with your decision-making process that you have to say, "Okay, maybe it's better if I scramble, or maybe it's better if I throw it away, or maybe it's better if I make a check-down." . . .

As a quarterback you have to be really smart about when you try to scramble or when you try to make a play, or sometimes it just happens very naturally . . . I'm really not trying to worry about that, as far as when I do what. It's not going out there and trying to take as many hits as possible. It's trying to be smart; it's going through my reads . . . If there are opportunities, then try to make a play.

—*"Denver Broncos Training Camp Quotes,"*
August 10, 2011

In Context

One of the criticisms directed toward Tebow is his penchant for running the ball, often in preference of passing.

He set an NFL record for most rushes (twenty-two) in one game by a quarterback, and in another game, he completed only two of eight pass attempts (the Broncos won both games, however). And yet, he also passed for 316 yards in the overtime playoff victory over the Pittsburgh Steelers.

Tebow is concerned with winning games—how he wins isn't as relevant to him. He adapts his play based on how the defense attacks him, and being a serious threat to run means that he keeps defenses guessing as to what he will do—run or pass? This defensive guessing game opens up opportunities: If Tebow can't find an open receiver, he'll look to run.

Adaptability—being able to get the job done no matter the circumstances—is a primary reason why the New York Jets traded for Tebow. They want to use his innovative playmaking ability to confuse defenses, and by employing him in the Wildcat offense, which is distinguished by a direct snap to the running back (in this case, Tebow), who can then hand off, run, or throw the ball, based on how the defense is set up.

ANXIETY

It's something I learned early on at Florida . . . if
you can't control it, don't worry about it.

—Press conference introducing Tebow as a New York Jet,
March 26, 2012

In Context

Tebow's unconventional quarterbacking style and his outspoken Christian faith have brought him criticism since early in his college football career. In interviews, he has consistently said that his response to things outside his control is to simply not worry about them, to the extent possible.

Rather, he focuses on what he *can* control, namely, staying focused on his goals and working hard to achieve them. That's what he did while the media rumors surrounding the Broncos' courting of Peyton Manning to replace him were swirling. Knowing he didn't have any control over what Denver was going to do, Tebow spent his time working out and practicing, ensuring that he would be in top form regardless of what happened.

ATTITUDE

※

It doesn't change my mind-set or my attitude or anything. It's just another opportunity and another challenge. Every day presents itself with enough of those. You just have to have a good attitude and approach it the right way.

—The New York Times *online, May 10, 2012*

In Context

Tebow explained how he will handle being the backup quarterback behind Mark Sanchez for the Jets, after having just completed a season as the starter for the Broncos.

Going from being the number one guy and playing the entire game to being number two and getting minimal playing time has to eat away at any true competitor, especially one as driven as Tebow.

Viewing this as an opportunity rather than a setback, however, Tebow reframes the situation in a positive way, and has set out to make the most of it by staying upbeat and working hard—enabling him to be ready to step up and perform when he does get a chance to play.

BEING A ROLE MODEL

⚛

All that it takes to be a role model is someone looking up to you. I think everyone to a certain extent is a role model because you either have your son, your daughter, a friend, a neighbor or someone looking at you and seeing how you respond to good, to bad, and how you handle yourself. There are some people who are more of a role model than others, but I really believe most people have someone looking at them, and that makes them a role model. They need to understand that and try to be the best role model they can because they can affect someone's life.

—New York Post *online, December 15, 2011*

In Context

Tebow wholeheartedly embraces being a role model. He views the public platform football gives him as a responsibility to set a strong moral standard for the many young people who look up to him because of his athletic ability

and accomplishments. Inspiring kids to emulate his positive beliefs and actions is more important to him than
achieving success on the football field.

He doesn't drink alcohol, in part because he doesn't
want kids to see him do that and then think it's cool and
begin drinking at a young age. His well-known decision
to wait for marriage before engaging in sexual activity is
a decision he hopes young people will also follow him in.

Tebow points out that most of us have someone who
looks up to us, and that we should govern our own behavior accordingly. In that sense, he is a role model to adults
as well—encouraging them to be role models to the people in their own circle of influence.

BELIEF

If you believe, then unbelievable things can
sometimes be possible.

—*Postgame press conference, Denver Broncos vs.*
Chicago Bears, December 11, 2011

In Context

Tebow made this statement after leading the Broncos to a 13–10 overtime victory against the Chicago Bears, despite having been down 10–0 late in the fourth quarter. He led the Broncos to five comeback victories in the 2011 regular season as well as the overtime victory in the playoffs against the league's top defense, the Pittsburgh Steelers.

He seems to always believe he has a chance to pull out a victory, no matter how tough the opponent, how far behind his team is, or how little time is left in the game. Tebow keeps playing hard and his belief in both himself and his teammates inspires a higher level of play that often brings about an unbelievable victory.

Biblical
Role Models

[David] had the courage to face Goliath when no one would do it. When David was older, he messed up along the way, but he repented and got back right. He was one of the greatest warriors of all time. God called David a man after his own heart.

Paul wasn't always a Christian. He persecuted Christians. But his faith became so strong, he was persecuted for it himself. Even when he was in prison and getting tortured, [Paul] pressed on for the cause. I spoke about him in Thailand [last week] because he showed great perseverance through hard times. That's why I looked up to him. He was never ashamed of his faith.

—The Florida Times-Union *online, July 3, 2008*

In Context

As a Christian, Tebow draws inspiration from godly examples set by believers in the Bible. In this quote, Tebow's mention of the Apostle Paul in particular stands out. Like Paul, Tebow perseveres through trials, such as working through his dyslexia (a reading disability that makes recognizing and processing certain symbols difficult), dealing with constant criticism for his style of play, winning games despite still developing his passing skills, and boldly proclaiming his faith in Christ in the face of much ridicule from detractors who mock him for being uptight and preachy.

Now, certainly, Tebow's trials are nothing compared to Paul's—Tebow hasn't been imprisoned and tortured for his beliefs (or for games when he completes 6 out of 22 passes for 60 yards)—but, like Paul, Tebow is never ashamed to express his faith in Jesus Christ, a stance that brings him substantial criticism and mockery in this pluralistic, relativistic age.

BRIGHTENING
SOMEONE'S DAY

We got to meet and hang out. I asked her if she
wanted to walk the red carpet with me, and so it
was fun. She went and got this dress.

—On the red carpet at the College Football Awards,
December 10, 2009

In Context

Kelly Faughnan is a brain tumor survivor whom Tebow
first met when she was twenty years old.

A huge Tebow fan, she had come to Orlando, Florida,
with her family in the hopes of meeting Tebow during
the College Football Awards. Upon meeting her by
chance at a restaurant the night before the ceremony,
Tebow invited her to accompany him as his date. Because
Faughnan still suffered from speech and balance issues,
their walk down the red carpet was slow, but deeply
meaningful and fun for both of them.

Tebow met with Faughnan again, after a 41–23 loss to
the New England Patriots late in the 2011 season. He said

meeting with her after the loss put things in perspective for him, as that setback was nothing compared to the struggles Faughnan has endured, and that being able to brighten her day lessened the sting of losing. Faughnan's father says Tebow's visits and encouragement have greatly lifted her spirits.

Character Formation

The two people that had the greatest impact on my life would be my parents, my mom and my dad, who taught me so many great things growing up and are constantly parenting me to this day.

And just from watching them, learning the character qualities, learning about the Bible, learning from my dad how to be a man, and learning from my mom how to be sweet and try to be caring to everybody that I meet. I'm constantly trying to learn and improve on all those things to this day.

—Jockey's "Timeout with Tebow: Video Series 4 of 6," December 26, 2011

In Context

Tebow's parents are his two biggest sources of inspiration. He, like his four older siblings (two sisters and two brothers), was homeschooled from kindergarten through high school, ensuring that his parents' influence over his life was thorough. Tebow's mother would often begin school days with a reading of the Psalm of the day or Proverb of the day.

His father is an ordained minister, and both parents have been Christian missionaries to the Philippines. Tebow inherited his father's fearlessness—Bob Tebow has said the greatest thing that could happen to him would be to be killed while preaching the Gospel—and his mother's tenderness, as he tries to be warm and kind to everyone he meets.

Tebow's devotion to the Gospel and to righteous living has clearly been derived from his parents, bringing to mind the admonition from Proverbs 22:6: "Train up a child in the way he should go; even when he is old he will not depart from it."

Compassion

Whether I'm working out or on the football field, I rely on my athletic ability. But millions of children in the developing world can't even walk, run, or play with their friends. That's why I'm partnering with CURE.

CURE works in the poorest countries around the world to bring healing to children in desperate need. They give kids the life-changing surgeries they need and share the healing power of the Gospel with them.

—CURE International website

In Context

Tebow is blessed with extraordinary physical stature and prowess, and he enjoys using his athletic ability in both working out and playing football. Because of his compassion toward children who can't do the same, his charity organization, the Tim Tebow Foundation, partners with CURE International, a nonprofit faith-based organization that operates hospitals and medical programs throughout the developing world.

As much as Tebow loves to play football, he loves to bring happiness and healing to suffering people even more. He uses his fame and resources to both bring attention to the needs of others and to help the needy.

The first major initiative Tebow and CURE are undertaking is the construction of a children's hospital in Davao City, Philippines. Focusing primarily on orthopedics, the hospital is expected to open in mid-2013.

COMPETITIVENESS

I don't like losing. Pretty much, every time I'm competing, I'll pretty much do whatever it takes to win. I'm pretty competitive.

—*ESPNNewYork.com, New York Jets blog,*
May 26, 2012

In Context

Tebow's competitive nature goes far beyond winning games—he wants to win at everything he competes in. Both with the Broncos and the Jets, teammates and reporters have commented on the fact that Tebow tries to outrun everyone else even in wind sprints during practice.

Some might perceive that to be petty or obsessive, but consider these two points:

One, it's Tebow's nature. He can't help but try to win in any competition (even if others don't recognize it as a competition); he has to prevail.

Two, high achievers don't slack off. They know that the competitive fire has to burn at all times—deciding to take it easy or figuring that it's okay to lose now and then, so long as it's not a "serious" competition, can breed a psychological acceptance of losing that could become the first, even if minor, degradation in their competitiveness.

Contentment

*A lot of people know Philippians 4:13 [NKJV]—"I
can do all things through Christ who strengthens
me"—but a lot of people don't interpret that verse
the right way. Most people think it means I can
do anything . . . on the football field, or I can
make a lot of money. But that's not exactly what
it's talking about there. It's [saying] I can be
content with anything. When you're a Christian,
you can [be content] because God has put you
where you are. That's really a different view . . .
I know that I have Christ in me, so I can do
whatever He wants me to do, and that's how I
approach everything.*

—Baptist Press, *September 21, 2009*

In Context

Philippians 4:13 has long been a favorite verse of athletes,
having essentially become a cliché. Many athletes refer
to it as a source of strength to draw upon in gaining confidence to perform well during a tough athletic trial,
which of course, it can be. However, as Tebow points out,

the verse is more about contentment than empowerment. It expresses the idea that Christ can enable a believer to be content no matter the circumstances.

This is clear by looking at the verse just prior, Philippians 4:12. The Apostle Paul says, "I know how to get along with humble means, and I also know how to live in prosperity; in any and every circumstance I have learned the secret of being filled and going hungry, both of having abundance and suffering need."

Tebow has tasted both athletic and financial success in America, but he has also spent several summers preaching and helping the needy in the Philippines, in very poor regions. He is familiar with both prosperity and poverty, and relies on Christ to grant him contentment and enjoyment in both instances.

CONTROLLING EMOTIONS

I'm a pretty amped up person and get hyped pretty easily and so I've always had to really try to stay calm before the storm and not get overhyped or too excited. That's just something that sometimes can come out in a game, but before the game and everything—just stay calm and go through everything that coaches want me to go through.

—*"Denver Broncos Training Camp Quotes,"*
August 12, 2010

In Context

Tebow's competitive excitement is evident in his outbursts of emotion on the field: throwing his hands up and yelling with joy after scoring, "Tebowing" in the end zone, stalking the sidelines with ferociousness as he exhorts his teammates to play hard.

As he says though, that's probably better suited for

during the game. Before it, he has to work at staying calm and focused.

A few of Tebow's pregame rituals, which help him focus:

- listening to calming music, such as Frank Sinatra and Chris Tomlin
- praying in the end zone
- doing hops before sprinting down the sideline.

Dealing with Critics

I can't control the naysayers. I can control my attitude and work ethic and determination and that's what I'm focused on now.

—MaxPreps.com, February 16, 2010

In Context

In both college and the NFL, Tebow has often been criticized both for the way he plays quarterback and for being so vocal about his Christian faith.

He hears the carping and it does affect him, but he tries to pay as little attention as possible to it. Not being able to control who says what about him, he chooses to focus instead on what he can control: his attitude, his work ethic, and his determination.

Tebow rarely, if ever, responds to his critics unless directly asked about them, and even then, he tends to say something positive about them before respectfully addressing the criticism.

Tebow's primary way of dealing with his critics seems to be to work as hard as possible to improve his skills and win games. Success on the field speaks louder to critics than just about anything he could say in his defense.

DECISION-MAKING

Quarterbacks fit all sizes and shapes. You're going to have quarterbacks that throw over the top, from the side. Quarterbacks that run, that are pocket passers. You're going to have all types of guys.

I think the biggest thing for a quarterback is just decision-making and being a leader out there in the field.

—The Palm Beach Post *online, October 20, 2011*

In Context

Tebow's style of play—he's a mobile quarterback who runs often and plows into defenders as he attempts to knock them out of his way—irritates and confounds many NFL analysts. How can he rush almost as much as he passes, have such mediocre (sometimes poor) passing statistics, play poorly for most of the game . . . and yet continue to win?

It shouldn't work, and it can't work for long, they say.

Except that, thus far, it has worked for Tebow. He

knows where his skill set lies and he emphasizes his strengths, getting the most out of them. Tebow's most important attribute, as he says here, is being a leader, by inspiring his teammates to play at a high level and making wise decisions on the field.

Determination

Things are going to be hard. There are so many obstacles. But if you already realize that and set in your mind that "Whatever comes my way, I'm going to overcome it" . . . you're going to finish strong, like we did in 2008 [at Florida] in winning the national championship.

—Winged Foot Scholar-Athlete Award banquet,
May 26, 2011

In Context

Tebow is incredibly determined to succeed at whatever he sets out to accomplish. In high school, he had a goal to win a state football championship: He did it, twice. In college, his goal was to win the national football championship: He did it, twice.

After college, his goal was to persuade just one NFL team to believe in him and draft him as a quarterback, despite many doubters: He did it, going in the first round to Denver. Once in the NFL, his goal was to become a starting quarterback: He did it, in his second year. Once he was the starter, his goal was to win games: He did it, taking the Broncos from last place in their division to first place and into the playoffs.

His mentality in the quote here boils down to a simple resolution: Refuse to lose.

ENJOYING LIFE

✳

If you're not enjoying life, then what are you doing? It doesn't matter how successful you are in whatever it is that you do, if you're not enjoying life you should change. I always try to have a smile on my face and try to brighten other people's days.

—Colorado AvidGolfer *online, September 12, 2011*

In Context

Many people slog through their days at jobs they hate or stay in unhealthy relationships. Others engage in medicative "hobbies" such as excessive drinking or find themselves watching hours of television every day, even though they may not really enjoy those things anymore—it's just been their daily routine for so long.

It's a cliché, but it's true: Life is short, far too short to spend it going around feeling miserable most of the time because you aren't willing to make positive changes.

Tebow himself clearly enjoys playing football. He also loves spreading God's message of salvation while meeting the needs of suffering people. He tries to make his mundane encounters with others positive, if just by smiling and being friendly to them.

Certainly, due to responsibilities and moral constraints, at times we must do things that aren't enjoyable, but that's not the same as going through life feeling miserable. As Tebow suggests, if you find you're not enjoying life, it's probably time to make some changes.

Expectations

That's something that I never have tried to do is live up to everyone's expectations of myself. I set high expectations for myself, and I try to live by them. That's why I put pressure on myself every day. That's why I work hard. That's why I try to improve every day because I have expectations for things that I want to accomplish.

—*"Denver Broncos News Release: Denver Broncos Quotes," October 11, 2011*

In Context

Tebow's not alone here. Many successful people—athletes, writers, musicians, preachers—have higher expectations for themselves than anyone else could ever have. They're their own harshest critics.

That internal drive toward excellence sets them apart. They're not that concerned with the expectations and pressure from others, because they're already working to meet their own higher expectations.

In Tebow's case, not only does he set high expectations for his football career, but also for the way he lives his life. His desire to be a role model for children necessitates that he acts with purpose, striving not just to do the right thing, but to do the righteous thing.

Eye Black
Scriptures

I was just putting on my eye black and I realized that if I put a Bible verse on it, somebody might actually get something out of it. It's just gained more and more momentum and steam, more and more people have recognized it, and now it's just got a life of its own.

—The Times-Picayune *(al.com), December 29, 2009*

In Context

In his junior year at Florida, Tebow began writing Scriptures from the Bible on his eye black (grease applied under the eyes to reduce sunlight glare). The first verse he chose was Philippians 4:13: "I can do all things through Him who strengthens me."

In the Gators' 24–14 victory over the Oklahoma Sooners in the 2009 BCS National Championship game, Tebow wore John 3:16: "For God so loved the world, that He gave His only begotten Son, that whoever believes in Him shall not perish, but have eternal life." During the game and the day after, John 3:16 was the top search phrase on Google, garnering more than 90 million searches.

Upon learning of that number, Tebow realized how immense a platform he had at Florida, and says it was a major factor in his choosing to return for his senior year.

Passionate for the Gospel, Tebow found an innovative way to spread the message to many people who might otherwise pay no attention to it.

Faith

To get me through? Without a doubt, one hundred percent. And that's the thing about my faith: it's not just something that happens when you're at church or happens when you're praying or reading the Scripture. It's part of who you are, as a person, as a player, in your life and everything.

—*Boston.com (Associated Press), December 14, 2011*

In Context

Tebow faces criticism from people who don't like his open espousal of Christianity, particularly his prayers on the football field and references to Jesus during postgame interviews.

But Tebow's faith is part of who he is—regardless of where he is. It's not relegated to church on Sundays, but informs and regulates his beliefs and behaviors in all of life.

Because Tebow's relationship with Jesus Christ is the focal point of his life and gives him such joy, he can't help but express that with regularity.

FIGHTING COMPLACENCY

We talk about it all the time. Complacency, leadership, not resting on your laurels, [don't] worry about what we did yesterday, but worry about how we can get better today. I think the number one way you counteract that is by every day you step in that weight room, every day you step on that practice field, you're worried about getting better and not getting by. . . .

Our focus is to get better every day. How can we be the best team, best player, best unit we can be . . . I think that's our mind-set. If we do that, I think we'll be successful.

—*2009 SEC Media Days, July 23, 2009*

In Context

Tebow explained how the Florida Gators intended to maintain a high level of play as they prepared for the upcoming season, having won the championship the year before.

Teams (and individuals) who achieve great success can find themselves coasting on their accomplishments and reputation. They can get complacent. The fire that previously burned within, provoking them to work hard and push themselves, wanes.

Tebow's advice to counteract and prevent that degradation in passion and commitment is simple: Focus on the here and now. Every moment that you're working on your craft, give it all you have.

Stay in the moment.

It's also great advice for simply enjoying life more—deciding to get the most out of whatever you're doing, wherever you are, and whomever you're with.

Finishing Strong

You need to finish what you start. You can't lose your passion or quit. No one wants to be around a quitter.

—Big Atlantic Classic tip-off banquet, January 31, 2010

In Context

Tebow constantly emphasizes the idea of finishing strong. It's central in his approach to success. It's not just a matter of keeping your word, though that's a huge part of it. It's also a recognition that while it's easy to start something, it's much harder to finish it, especially if the task is of any significance or requires sustained hard work. How many people start New Year's resolutions that never get fulfilled?

Tebow's point that we don't think highly of quitters is spot on. We have an almost instinctive revulsion to quitters, yet how often do we quit on our own goals? Tebow once told a fan on Twitter that the key to his success is that he's never quit anything that he started.

First Impressions

I'm going to be there early—as in "crack-of dawn" early. This is what I've been waiting for since the trade happened, and I want to make a good impression.

—New York Post *online, April 15, 2012*

In Context

Tebow was determined to attend the Jets' voluntary off-season program on the first day their training facility opened, and he wanted to be there early.

Being a newcomer to the Jets and bringing a lot of hype and controversy, Tebow knows that he has to prove himself to be a strong football player and good teammate rather than simply the ringleader of a media circus.

Showing up early on the first day of *voluntary* workouts sets a strong tone from the outset.

Fitness

As a football player and as an athlete, I'm someone who goes extremely hard, and so I need to train extremely hard and constantly keep going and I don't want a lot of rest because I want to be able to go-go-go in the games and when other teams and other players get tired, I want to be able to be at my peak and keep going.

—Stack TV: *"Tim Tebow's NFL Off-Season Workout,"*
February 1, 2012

In Context

Tebow's commitment to physical fitness began as a boy. He grew up on a farm doing manual labor and wanted to lift weights as soon as his parents would let him.

His size, strength, and stamina are crucial to his quarterbacking style, which is very physical. Tebow runs the ball often, and unlike typical quarterbacks who scramble for a few yards before sliding or running out-of-bounds, he runs right at defenders, lowering his shoulders to smash into them to fight for extra yards.

He wants to be in top physical form at the end of

games, when his superior fitness can give him an advantage over defenders who are losing steam.

Tebow told *Stack TV* that he does lots of explosive exercises, such as squat jumps and sled pulls, because he wants to maintain a powerful first step, which can get him past defenders.

Focus

We talked about it every day. That was our goal.
Every day was working toward a state
championship.

—The St. Augustine Record *online, December 25, 2005*

In Context

Tebow led Nease High School to a 44–37 victory over Seffner Armwood in the Class 4A Florida state high school football championship. It was Nease's first-ever championship.

As a high school senior, Tebow was already receiving plenty of national media attention for his football exploits. He was featured in an ESPN documentary titled *Tim Tebow: The Chosen One* that followed him through his senior college year; the documentary reported that Tebow had eighty football scholarship offers.

Despite the crush of attention, Tebow stayed focused on the more immediate goal of winning a state championship, reminding himself and his teammates of it every day. The laser-like focus paid off when they won.

Football
Role Model

*I looked up to him, not really for how he played
on the field, but for how he handled himself
off of it. Danny [Wuerffel] set a great example
for a six-year-old boy. He was someone who
was humble and who could handle victory
and defeat.*

—Sharing the Victory, *August/September 2009*

In Context

Part of Tebow's desire to be a role model stems from the influence of his own football role model, Danny Wuerffel, who was the quarterback of the Florida Gators from 1993 to 1996, when Tebow was a boy. Like Tebow, Wuerffel won the Heisman Trophy and a national championship. He is also a committed Christian. As a boy, Tebow stood in line to get Wuerffel's autograph and Wuerffel's graciousness toward him left a lasting impression.

While he was at Florida, Tebow won the All Sports

Association's 2008 Wuerffel Trophy, a national award honoring the college football player who best combines community service with academic and athletic excellence.

GETTING
BACK UP

*You can't lose confidence in yourself, or you've
lost already. When you get knocked down, you've
got to keep getting back up.*

—New York Post *online (Associated Press),*
October 24, 2011

In Context

Tebow said this following his first game as starting quarterback for the Broncos in 2011.

He played horribly for most of the game and was
heckled by fans. When the Broncos got the ball back at
their 20-yard line with less than five and a half minutes
remaining, they were losing to the Miami Dolphins,
15–0. Tebow had only completed 4 passes out of 14 attempts for 40 yards.

And then . . . Tebow threw a touchdown pass to cut
the deficit to 15–7. The Broncos recovered the onside
kick. Tebow threw another touchdown pass to make the

score 15–13. He then ran in a two-point conversion to tie the game at 15–15.

In overtime, Denver recovered a Miami fumble, and a few plays later, Matt Prater kicked a 52-yard field goal to give the Broncos an 18–15 victory.

GIVING GOD
THE GLORY

[M]y relationship with Jesus Christ is . . . the most important thing in my life. So any time I get an opportunity to tell Him that I love Him or [I'm] given an opportunity to shout Him out on national TV, I'm gonna take that opportunity . . . And then right after I give Him the honor and glory, I always try to give my teammates the honor and glory. . . .

I respect Jake [Plummer's] opinion, and I really appreciate his compliment of calling me a winner. But I feel like anytime I get the opportunity to give the Lord some praise, He is due for it because of what He did for me and what He did on the cross for all of us.

—ESPN First Take, *November 22, 2011*

In Context

Tebow explained why he frequently talks about Jesus in interviews. He was responding to former Denver Broncos quarterback Jake Plummer, who praised Tebow as a winner but also criticized him for constantly talking about Jesus Christ. Plummer said he would like Tebow better if he didn't have to hear about Tebow's love for the Lord after every game.

Tebow's response was gracious and he didn't say anything negative about Plummer. He clearly disagreed with Plummer, but instead of getting vindictive, he took the opportunity to lay out why he is so vocal about his faith—because of "what He [Jesus] did on the cross for all of us," that is, make peace between sinful humans and a holy God.

God's Sovereignty

No matter where I am, if I'm preaching to Muslims or in a prison, if you're in the will of God, that's safer than driving down the interstate. That's how I feel about it. He's in control of whatever happens. I'm thinking more about their needs than my needs. They need to hear what I'm sharing, so I don't think about any sense of fear. The Lord has it under control, and he'll take care of me.

—*ESPN.com, May 5, 2008*

In Context

Tebow explained why he isn't afraid to go into prisons in America and preach to violent criminals or go to the Philippines and preach to Muslims—because God is "in control of whatever happens." Trusting God to take care of him, Tebow goes forth doing what he believes is the will of God for his life.

He believes that the message of the Gospel is the most important thing anyone can hear, and he wants to use his platform as a popular athlete to open doors so that he can spread that message. Even to people who might be hostile towards it.

Tebow has been visiting prisons since early in his college football career, and he has gone to the Philippines several times, beginning when he was fifteen years old.

GOING HARD

I love playing football so much, and if you love doing something, you can't not go as hard as you can. If I ever went out there and didn't give one hundred percent, I'd feel bad. It's worse than what anybody else can say to me. It's inside me. I just grew up with that type of learning and that type of character.

—*Gator Bait Magazine's* Florida Football 2007
preseason yearbook

In Context

Tebow holds himself to a higher standard of excellence than anyone else does. It's why he's so emotional on the field, because he's going hard on every play.

This is evident by how hard he works to keep plays alive and how difficult it is for defenders to tackle him once he takes off running.

Teammates in college and the NFL have remarked about how hard Tebow trains in the weight room, and his high school football coach said that for Tebow, every game is the Super Bowl.

Graciousness

I will always be grateful to the Broncos organization for giving me the initial opportunity to fulfill my dream of being an NFL quarterback.

—Twitter: @TimTebow, March 29, 2012

In Context

Two months prior to making this statement, Tebow had just finished a season that reenergized the Broncos franchise. He led the team from last place in their division to first, into the playoffs, and to an overtime victory in the first round of the playoffs. Tebow and the Broncos were the talk of the NFL. Broncos executive vice president John Elway declared that Tebow had earned the right to be the starting quarterback going into training camp for the upcoming season.

Shortly after, however, Peyton Manning became a free agent, and the Broncos openly courted him. They ultimately signed Manning to be their new starting quarterback. The Broncos then traded Tebow to the New

York Jets, where he would be the backup quarterback to Mark Sanchez.

If Tebow had any anger or resentment over being dismissed so quickly after having given Denver such a successful and exciting season, he didn't take it public. Instead of lashing out at the Broncos in the media over how they treated him, Tebow simply and graciously expressed appreciation to the Broncos for giving him an opportunity to begin his NFL career. Elway remarked that Tebow handled the situation with class.

Handling Fame

With everything, there are pros and cons . . . It's an honor that people want to talk to you and get your autograph and take pictures . . . But sometimes it is nice when you can just go out to dinner with your family and spend time with them. You never really get to see them and when you are with them and you go out to eat or something, you're signing a lot of the time.

[S]omething that helps me handle it is knowing that I was a kid once and I looked up to Danny Wuerffel, and when he signed an autograph for me, it made me feel good . . . you're helping other people, and that's what it's all about.

—Sports Illustrated *online, Inside College Football column, December 7, 2007*

In Context

Tebow said this in his second year of college; imagine how much more attention he encounters now that he's in the NFL and has unleashed Tebow mania on the nation.

Tebow's boyhood meeting with his football hero, Danny Wuerffel, was influential in shaping his attitude toward how he deals with children who constantly want to talk to him or get his autograph. Tebow was one of the last kids in line to meet Wuerffel, but Wuerffel still treated Tebow with warmth.

Moreover, Tebow takes advantage of his fame by using it as a vehicle to pursue his humanitarian aims—visiting with sick children and prisoners, and preaching the Gospel and giving motivational speeches to groups around the country.

Hard Work

A quote that I've always lived by, that's been at my door since I was six years old, is "Hard work beats talent when talent doesn't work hard." So every day, I'm trying to go out there and outwork everybody else. It doesn't matter if you're more talented and more blessed than me, I'm going to outwork you every day of the week.

—Tampa Bay Times, *April 23, 2010*

In Context

Tebow knows his passing skills aren't as polished as those of many other quarterbacks, but he also knows that few people are willing to work as hard as he is to get better.

What Tebow lacks in skill, he makes up for in hard work.

Coaches and reporters have observed that Tebow is the first player on the practice field and the last player off it. Almost everyone who has observed him, even people who don't think Tebow is, or can be, a good player, praises his work ethic.

How to Improve America

First and foremost is what this country was based on . . . one nation under God. And the more that we can get back to that, I believe the better we'll be.

—*"Easter on the Hill" service, Georgetown, Texas,*
April 8, 2012

In Context

At an outdoor Easter service that drew 15,000 people, Tebow gave his view on where America most needs to be changed.

Tebow is doing his part to effect that change by proclaiming the Gospel with regularity and being a role model for young people. He said his prayer is that God will raise up more athletes who embrace being a role model.

However, politics may be in his future as well. He has said that running for political office is something he prays about.

How to Succeed

Whatever you're doing, put everything into it. Put your whole heart into it and you're going to get something out of it. So if you really want to become your best, push yourself in whatever you're doing as hard as you possibly can and you will find results.

—Stack TV: *"Tim Tebow's NFL Off-Season Workout,"*
February 1, 2012

In Context

Putting everything he has into his endeavors appears to be an obsession for Tebow. It's a healthy obsession, though, that fits with his goal to work harder than anybody else at whatever it is he's competing in.

When Tebow says you will achieve results in your projects if you put everything you have into them, he speaks from experience: He's won at every level of football, from high school to college to the NFL.

HUMILITY

I remind myself all the time to stay humble. I'm not going to change because of all this (attention). I'm just not going to do it.

—St. Petersburg Times *online, December 9, 2005*

In Context

Tebow said this as he was finishing his senior year of high school. He was experiencing major attention from the media and college football programs, having set numerous records and won several awards—he was named Florida's player of the year in 2004 and 2005. The ESPN documentary about him would air within a week of this interview.

Despite going on to even greater football success and media attention in college and the NFL, Tebow has stayed true to his early commitment to humility. He doesn't brag, preferring to praise his teammates and coaches rather than discuss himself.

A story he often tells sheds light on the source of his humility.

When Tebow was a boy and he and his older brothers

began experiencing athletic success, their parents instituted a humility rule: The boys could not talk about how
well they played in a game unless first asked about it by
someone else. Tebow says it was a great lesson in learning
to not be so quick to talk about himself.

Ignoring
Distractions

*I've never really listened to outside
distractions . . . you're always going to have
people talking, you're always going to have
naysayers and critics and haters. And for me I
can't let that affect me. I have to wake up every
morning with goals in my mind of how I want
to approach the day and stay focused, stay
positive, and have a great mind-set and try
to be a great teammate.*

—*"Face to Face: Tim Tebow," ESPN, February 3, 2012*

In Context

Tebow explained how he was able to tune out the constant media scrutiny he faced as his popularity grew
with the Denver Broncos in 2011. Each comeback victory
that he engineered (five in the regular season) brought
more and more attention.

The attention wasn't all positive, as critics piled on
daily about his style of play, his throwing motion, his

"Tebowing," his praising of the Lord, and basically his audacity to try to be an NFL quarterback.

However, Tebow recognizes that he can't control what someone he's never met is going to say about him, so why stress over it? What he can do is stay focused on his clear goals for each day and work as hard as he can to achieve them.

INFLUENCE

How you are going to influence someone is they see something in you that is different or seems special. They see something in you that they think, "Wow, that's really cool. I'm going to look into that," or maybe, "He's nice about this. He goes about this a different way," and then they'll look into it. But it's not because I'm forcing anything upon anyone.

I try to make [faith] a part of my life, just like it is. And I will never deny or force it. But I will always have it as a part of my life . . . I hope that people can see it affects my life and how I am so passionate about it, and that's the biggest effect I hope that people see.

—The Florida Times-Union *online, November 27, 2009*

In Context

Tebow is not a fire-and-brimstone type of Christian. Nor does he act self-righteously or preach to people in a heavy-handed way.

Rather, he's humble and friendly, while boldly proclaiming his faith in Christ. His approach calls to mind 1 Peter 3:15: "[B]ut sanctify Christ as Lord in your hearts, always being ready to make a defense to everyone who asks you to give an account for the hope that is in you, yet with gentleness and reverence."

Tebow's influence flows from his behavior. People see him playing hard and always competing, exuding humility and congeniality, and spending time and money to help suffering people. They see how much joy and purpose his faith in Christ gives him. Because of these things, some unbelievers may find themselves drawn to the same faith, or at least take its claims more seriously.

Intangibles

The number one thing that you can't teach is leadership, winning and competitiveness. Will I work at stuff for the next level? Yes. But you know what, I would rather want a coach that wants me for me. For those three things.

—The Quad: The New York Times College Sports Blog,
August 28, 2009

In Context

As a college senior, Tebow was asked what areas of his game he needed to work on to improve his NFL draft prospects. He mentioned footwork and decision-making, but then made it clear that what really matters for success as a player are the intangibles: leadership, winning, and competitiveness.

While Tebow's quarterbacking is unconventional and his passing skills are frequently criticized, even his critics are forced to acknowledge that few players are as competitive as he is, and that he is an inspirational leader. And so far, Tebow has also won lots of games.

Integrity

*I endorse something because I believe in it. I
endorse pro-life for the same reason. I believe in
it. When people see me talking about something,
they know it's not because I'm just getting paid
for it. My integrity means more to me than any
fame or money. When I say something, I want
people to take it to the bank that I mean it and
believe in it.*

—The Florida Times-Union *online, February 21, 2011*

In Context

Tebow endorses Nike, Jockey, and FRS. He chooses his
endorsements based upon whether the products are
something he actually uses and believes in, and if the
company fits with his character.

For example, while he was training for the NFL draft,
he began drinking FRS Healthy Energy drink several
times a day. FRS saw Tebow drinking it at the NFL combine, and then approached him for an endorsement deal.

Intensity

It's not just playing hard, but playing harder with a focus and determination of what you're doing every play. Not just going full speed, but going full speed to dominate. Playing with anger somewhat, playing with intensity, with passion. You can only go so hard with natural ability.

—Orlando Sentinel *online, November 1, 2008*

In Context

Tebow's intensity manifests itself in his vocal and emotional demeanor on the field. But it's much more than that. He admits to "playing with anger," which could mean anger at the last loss or the most recent bad play; it could also mean anger at the constant barrage of criticism he faces.

Whatever the source and focus of his anger, Tebow harnesses it to motivate him to play even harder than his own fiercely competitive nature already drives him to, but it isn't simply a wild "going all-out" approach; it's a clearly focused determination of what has to be done in order to not just win, but to dominate.

Jesus Christ

[T]he exciting thing about having a relationship with Christ, is we're not perfect and we never will be. But Jesus Christ is perfect, and He died on a cross for our sins and He rose again, and because He has the power to defeat death, He has the power to give you eternal life, and He is offering it to you as a free gift. That means you cannot work for it, you cannot pay for it, you cannot be good enough for it. The only thing you can do is accept it.

—*"Easter on the Hill" service, Georgetown, Texas,*
April 8, 2012

In Context

Tebow prayed to accept Jesus Christ as his Lord and Savior as a young boy, and he says it is the most important thing that ever happened in his life. This is why he speaks about Christ often.

Tebow wants others to experience the same peace and reconciliation with God that he has, both now on earth and later in heaven.

Some people may look at Tebow's apparently impeccable morality and behavior and conclude that their life doesn't measure up to his, that they just aren't good enough for Christ.

But Tebow acknowledges that he isn't perfect; in fact, he says none of us ever will be. As Jesus said in Mark 2:17, "It is not those who are healthy who need a physician, but those who are sick; I did not come to call the righteous, but sinners."

LEADERSHIP

Everyone will follow the leaders. If the leaders aren't complacent, if the leaders still have their edge, if they're still pushing, if they still have that desire, that discipline, that devotion, then everybody else will because they're going to follow the leader.

As a leader, we just have to make sure that every day you come in with an edge, that desire, that hunger, and everybody is going to feed off of that. The team will have that desire, that hunger.

—USA TODAY *online, July 28, 2009*

In Context

Tebow said this in the summer before his senior year at Florida, with the Gators having just won the prior year's national championship, and looking to repeat. They would not win the title again, although they came very close, ending the season with a 13–1 record and ranking number three in the polls. The only team they lost to, Alabama, was the eventual national champion.

Tebow recognizes that in any organization, the leaders set the tone. Only if the leaders work hard and demand excellence from themselves, demonstrating that devotion every day through their actions, can they inspire the rest of team to do the same.

Alternatively, weak leaders, leaders who don't push hard, who don't do their best every time, will breed laziness and lack of commitment.

LEARNING FROM FAILURE

I feel like I usually let stuff go pretty well, but I don't know if you always want to. It's a part of being motivated. It's learning from mistakes, learning from past failures, and also learning from losses and having that feeling of disappointment drive you in practice and meetings to watch more, do more. I don't know if you always want to just let things go and just continue to be the same person. I think you need to let it eat at you a little bit because I think that can make you better as a player, as a person.

—*"Denver Broncos News Release: Denver Broncos Quotes," December 28, 2011*

In Context

When Tebow said this, the Broncos were in the midst of a three-game losing streak to end the 2011 season and seeing their playoff hopes dissipate. They ended up backing into the playoffs by default, due to divisional tiebreakers.

Tebow and the Broncos bounced back in the first round of the playoffs, beating the Pittsburgh Steelers in overtime.

While it's wise to not obsess over failures and to always move forward, Tebow knows that feeling the pain and experiencing the anger of failing can drive us to put in more work and sharpen our focus to do better next time.

Legacy

Because it's one thing to score touchdowns and win trophies and championships, but at the end of the day that doesn't matter. But if you can affect people, if you can change people's lives, if you can be a good role model, someone that a mom or dad can look to their son and say, "Hey, that's how you need to handle it," then that's my ultimate goal. And that's ultimately how I would define my life as having success if I can reach that.

—Hannity, *Fox News Channel, May 31, 2011*

In Context

Few people are as driven to win as Tebow is, and his work ethic demonstrates that. But he is even more concerned with being a good role model for kids and improving the lives of others through his foundation's charity work.

Success to Tebow is leaving a legacy of uplifting others and helping them to succeed in their own lives in their own ways more so than achieving his own athletic acclaim.

LIVING BY FAITH

People have to realize that just because you're a Christian, it doesn't mean that you're perfect, because every once in a while everyone stumbles. Living by faith is about when you do mess up, getting back up, brushing yourself off, and keep trying to improve where you mess up or where you have temptation. I screw up all the time. I'm not saying you have to be perfect because you can't, but our goal is just trying to improve.

—Christianity Today *online, June 10, 2011*

In Context

Reporters often ask Tebow if he has any vices, because he appears "too good to be true"—a young professional athlete who doesn't drink, who is remaining abstinent until marriage, and who spends much time and many resources improving the lives of sick children and orphans.

He's responded by saying that he cracks his knuckles too much or forgets to put up his dishes after eating—is he being serious or making light of his reputation, or both?

Regardless, Tebow knows how he is perceived, and yet he makes it clear that he screws up "all the time."

No one is perfect, not even Tim Tebow, and the goal as a Christian, he says, is that when you do sin, you make things right and then move forward.

Living in Light of Eternity

I'm very competitive, and I want to win that championship, and I want to win the Heisman again, but it really doesn't matter because I'm focused on eternity and winning more important prizes—winning rewards in heaven.

—Charisma *online, September 30, 2008*

In Context

Tebow recognizes that rewards in heaven are eternal while rewards on earth are temporal.

As much as he wants to succeed in earthly pursuits, such as winning football games, he more so wants to lay the groundwork for prizes in heaven.

Tebow believes he earns eternal rewards by believing in Christ, following God's will for his life, preaching the Gospel, and helping the sick and needy.

Living with Passion

Whatever you do, do wholeheartedly unto the Lord . . . When you live with passion and you're enthusiastic about what you do, it's contagious. People want to have that. They're drawn to that. That's something my dad taught me when I was a little boy, is that's something you can do to separate yourself.

—*"Don Meyer Evening of Excellence," Lipscomb University, April 17, 2010*

In Context

Tebow is referencing Colossians 3:23–24: "Whatever you do, do your work heartily, as for the Lord rather than for men, knowing that from the Lord you will receive the reward of the inheritance. It is the Lord Christ whom you serve."

Tebow believes he isn't just working for his coaches and teammates—he's working for the Lord; he isn't just serving sick children and orphans—he's serving the Lord. This eternal perspective imbues him with a sense of mission that motivates him to live with passion, to go hard in everything he does so that he can fulfill his sense of divine calling.

Tebow seems to really embrace the idea of "Wherever you are, be all there" (a quote from the late missionary Jim Elliot), an attitude that can make all of life much more enjoyable and satisfying.

LOSING

It puts things in perspective. God is still God. I still have a relationship with Christ, and a loss doesn't change anything. Win or lose, everything is still the same. What matters is the girl I'm about to see, Kelly Faughnan. If I can inspire hope in someone, then it's still a good day.

—NFL.com, December 19, 2011

In Context

After a 41–23 loss to the New England Patriots (a game that had been hyped all week prior as Tim Tebow versus Tom Brady), Tebow met with Kelly Faughnan, a brain tumor survivor. Faughnan was Tebow's date to the College Football Awards two years before this meeting.

Tebow routinely responds to losses by telling reporters that even though he might have had a bad day on the football field, it's still a good day for him because he got to meet with a sick child and brighten his or her day. Tebow meets with sick children (and sometimes adults) before and after each game he plays, whether at home or on the road.

Tebow hates losing, but keeps it in proper perspective—God is still in control and he still has his saving relationship with Christ. This mentality enables Tebow to more readily move on from losses and bad games, and thus remain positive and focused to play better next time.

MAKING
SACRIFICES

You know, everybody, they can see, they can look and see how easy it is. But it's definitely not that easy. The difference is 'cause not many people want to wake up at 5:00, go through workouts, go speak to young kids, go back, eat lunch, go to class, go to tutoring, go speak at a prison at night, come back. I mean, more people would do those things; they just don't want to sacrifice.

—2008 SEC Media Days, July 23, 2008

In Context

A reporter, referencing Tebow's football success, charitable works, positive attitude, and strong morality, asked him if his life was on "cruise control." Tebow responded that it definitely isn't.

The reason it might appear that way to outsiders is because they only see the outward manifestations of his success.

But they don't see all the sacrifices Tebow makes in order to accomplish these goals, sacrifices that take up time and energy, such as getting by on less sleep or sticking to a regimented schedule that allows little free time.

Modesty

I'm sure someone kept the stats, but I haven't kept track.

—Baptist Press, *January 24, 2006*

In Context

As he began his college football career, Tebow was asked to reflect on the details of his many high school football records: He couldn't do it.

Tebow's parents counseled him to abide by the ethos of Proverbs 27:2: "Let another praise you, and not your own mouth; a stranger, and not your own lips."

They discouraged him from reading media accounts of his athletic accomplishments.

The Tebows' goal was not to denigrate or minimize their son's success, but rather to keep him level-headed, to encourage him to develop humility.

It appears to have worked, as Tebow is rarely if ever caught bragging about himself. Instead he maintains a modest demeanor that ingratiates him even to fans of opposing teams.

MOST IMPORTANT THING IN LIFE

I'm a Christian, I'm a follower of Jesus Christ, and that is first and foremost the most important thing in my life.

—*Press conference introducing Tebow as a New York Jet, March 26, 2012*

In Context

Tebow makes it clear that nothing matters more to him than his relationship with Jesus Christ, that his belief in Christ as the Lord and Savior of his life is by far the greatest thing that has ever happened to him.

Tebow gave this answer to a reporter who asked what exactly he believes in terms of his oft-referenced faith. The reporter also wondered about Tebow's views on hot-button social and political issues.

Tebow refused to get caught up in individual issues of controversy, and instead directed the focus of his beliefs to "the most important thing," his relationship with Jesus Christ.

MOTIVATION

When people see the work ethic, determination and the passion that I have, they're going to ask, "What drives you? What is that?" Well, the answer is my relationship with Jesus Christ. That's just what has always fueled me.

—Sharing the Victory, *August/September 2009*

In Context

Because it's the most important thing in his life, Tebow's relationship with Jesus Christ is also his ultimate motivation for working hard, staying focused, and pursuing his goals with passion.

Tebow believes that since Christ gave His all—His very life—on the cross to atone for his sins and make peace with a holy God for him, he then should also give his all in whatever God calls him to do, be that football or humanitarianism.

This ties in with Tebow's approach to influence: By demonstrating a strong work ethic and passion for winning, people will inevitably ask him the source of it all. He can then talk about Christ in response.

Moving Forward

I know that everything happened for a reason. And I'm not someone that looks back or asks why or anything like that. I just look forward and figure out how I can make the most of every opportunity and how can I make the most of being a New York Jet.

—The Michael Kay Show, *March 30, 2012*

In Context

In January 2012, Tebow completed a magical season with the Denver Broncos, having led them from last place in their division to a first round victory in the playoffs.

Two months later, the Broncos thanked Tebow for his efforts by signing Peyton Manning to replace him and then trading him away to the New York Jets.

Before the trade, Tebow had talked about how he was looking forward to working with John Elway in the off-season to improve his quarterbacking and his desire to bring more success to Denver next year.

And then . . . he was gone. All of those plans went out

the window. He found himself with a new team, having gone from being a starter to being a backup.

Instead of looking back and getting angry or feeling dejected, Tebow moved forward and set about the business of making the most of the opportunity he's been given in New York.

NEVER GIVING UP

Any time you're getting beaten like that you just continue to fight. It doesn't change who you are, how you play, how you go out there—you should be the same at all times. That's what I wanted to show and it didn't matter if it was the first play or the last play or if we were down by 42, I was going to be the same player and I was going to still give everything I have because that's all I have to give. Every time I step on the field I'm going to give my whole heart regardless of the score.

—Post-game press conference, Denver Broncos vs. New England Patriots, January 14, 2012

In Context

Tebow continued to play hard late in the game during Denver's 45–10 loss to the New England Patriots in the second round of the 2011–12 NFL playoffs.

His stats on the day were poor: He completed 9 passes out of 26 attempts for 136 yards and no touchdowns.

Tebow's never-give-up attitude didn't pull out a dramatic comeback victory this time (positivity and hustle aren't magic), and with just minutes remaining and the Broncos down several touchdowns, Tebow had to know they were going to lose.

But his mentality is that "you should be the same at all times," that no matter the score, no matter how much time is left in the game, you should always give it your all when you step on the field and compete.

A determination to always work your hardest, to always do your best, and to never give up won't always net you a victory, but it often will—Tebow did lead the Broncos to five comeback victories in the regular season and an overtime playoff win, after all.

Nutrition

It all starts with your diet. So, number one is eating a great breakfast. A lot of egg whites, probably a Myoplex shake, and then oatmeal or grits, something like that for carbs.

—Stack TV: *"Tim Tebow Trains for the NFL,"*
June 8, 2010

In Context

Tebow is a huge believer in the benefits of eating healthy. His mother says that as a boy, he was so committed to building his body that he eschewed junk food on his own. In his autobiography, Tebow tells the story of how in middle school, he went an entire year without drinking soft drinks in order to win $100 from his parents—and says he still does not drink them.

Men's Health reported that, in college, Tebow drank cherry juice before and after lifting weights, because it contains a healthy mixture of carbohydrates and protein.

The reason why Tebow endorses FRS Healthy Energy drinks is that the company spotted him drinking them on TV during the NFL combine and then offered him a contract. Tebow relied upon the healthy energy drink, which is low in sugar and high in antioxidants, to keep his immune system strong during training because he was running on low sleep for sustained periods.

Tebow has long loved vanilla ice cream, but minimizes his consumption of it to about once a week.

In short, nutrition is a key component of Tebow's extraordinary physical strength and energy, and it has been since he was young.

Orphans

My number one heart is with orphans. The foundation supports 600 orphans in different places around the world. That's what I want to do for a long time and make it bigger. I want to support kids that not a lot of people believe in. Give them an opportunity to do good in school, play sports, and get scholarships.

—The Florida Times-Union *online, February 21, 2011*

In Context

James 1:27 is relevant here: "Pure and undefiled religion in the sight of our God and Father is this: to visit orphans and widows in their distress, and to keep oneself unstained by the world."

In 1992, Tebow's father's ministry, the Bob Tebow Evangelistic Association (BTEA), founded an orphanage in the Philippines. Later, the orphanage was named Uncle Dick's Home in honor of Richard Fowler, a neighbor of the Tebows in Jacksonville, Florida, known as "Uncle Dick" to the Tebow children. The Tebows led Fowler to Christ, and he became a supporter of the

BTEA, leaving money to be used after his death to support the orphanage.

The Tim Tebow Foundation, Tebow's own charity organization, partners with Uncle Dick's Home and other orphanages around the world. When Tebow was in high school, he traveled with his father to the Philippines and visited with the orphans, ministering to them. While there, he developed a heart for orphans and has made their cause his cause.

Passion for Goals

Passion is not adrenaline . . . Passion is when you don't want to stay up late studying but you do. Passion is something that comes from deep down inside. It is not when I'm on the field and I throw my arms up [in celebration]. That's adrenaline. Passion is all the nights you can't see me working. Passion is all the nights you stay up training for your football game. Passion is when you're tired and still doing what you know is right and what needs to be done. That's passion.

—*Winged Foot Scholar-Athlete Award banquet,*
May 26, 2011

In Context

Tebow makes an insightful distinction between passion and adrenaline. Adrenaline manifests itself in emotional excitement over success, while passion is what brings about that success, by motivating us to work on our goals when it's hard and we don't feel like it.

Passion for winning is why Tebow is so committed to outworking his opponents, why he works out so hard, why he eats such a disciplined diet, and why he is so obsessed with finishing strong in everything he begins.

Passion for the Gospel

Shouldn't we be as passionate about the greatest gift of all—Jesus—as we are about football? God gave us His Son, an abundant life and if you can't be passionate about that, I don't know what you can be passionate about.

But we are not passionate about sharing it and that's pretty disappointing. We talk about football or the movies we see. Why wouldn't you talk about the love of Jesus Christ?

—First Redeemer Church, Cumming, Georgia, July 4, 2010

In Context

As passionate as Tebow is about winning football games, he is even more passionate about winning souls for Jesus Christ.

Because he is so successful in football and so demon-

strably passionate about it, when he takes people to task
for loving football more than Jesus, his critique stings
and penetrates more than it might from a typical
preacher.

PATIENCE

I think, when I was in the Philippines and watched all those people going about their business without stuff we just took for granted, I learned patience. So it didn't matter where I went, just so I went. If it was [Friday], and the second round or so, then so be it. But I am glad that it's over.

—*ESPN.com, April 22, 2010*

In Context

Tebow was not expected by most analysts to be drafted in the first round of the 2010 NFL draft, although he himself believed he had a shot at doing so.

Ultimately, the Denver Broncos selected Tebow with the 25th pick in the first round.

Tebow noted that the uncertainty of which team would pick him and when, did make him anxious ("I am glad that it's over"); however, his trips to the Philippines with his father's ministry taught him patience and perspective, which helped him deal with the stress of it all.

Observing people in the Philippines living daily without many of the luxuries, comforts, and even necessities that Americans take for granted gave Tebow an appreciation for what really matters. Where he would be picked in the NFL draft is important, but it's nowhere near as significant or stressful as waking up each day trying to figure out where to find something to eat.

Perseverance

*It's not what you do when you're up. It's what you
do when you're down. That's what guys look at
you for—how you handle it when something goes
wrong. That's everything. That's playing
through adversity, that's perseverance, that's
determination. That's all the character qualities
you want. Coming back from those hard times,
that's what makes you who you are.*

—Men's Fitness, *September 2008*

In Context

A classic example of Tebow's perseverance occurred
shortly after this interview with *Men's Fitness* was published:

After a 31–30 upset loss to Ole Miss early in the 2008
season, a season in which Florida had been determined
to go undefeated, Tebow sat in the locker room for a long
time, filled with anger and sadness.

When he finally emerged to speak to reporters, he
apologized to Gator fans and promised them that he and

the rest of the team would work harder than any other player and team in the nation for the rest of the season. Inspired by Tebow's determination and leadership, Florida went on to win the rest of their regular season games and the national championship.

PERSPECTIVE—
IT'S JUST A GAME

I get asked all the time about pressure. You know, "Timmy, how are you going to handle the pressure of trying to repeat as national champs or trying to win the Heisman again?" But pressure is when you're fighting for your life in the hospital or for your next meal. There are millions of people who haven't eaten in three days. Me? I'm playing a game I love, and people happen to be watching. That's not pressure.

—ESPN The Magazine, *September 21, 2009*

In Context

Tebow's travels to the Philippines and his visits with sick children have granted him a realistic perspective of pressure. People fighting for their lives or struggling with hunger face real pressure; the pressure that football players face to perform is real, but in comparison, the consequences are nil.

If a football player doesn't win a game or an award,

he's still got his health and his access to resources (in most cases), but health and hunger issues can have far more devastating outcomes.

Tebow's ability to put pressure in its proper perspective likely helps him to navigate all of the expectations and criticism he faces, and simply focus on playing football. This increases his chances for success, as the distractions of "pressure" don't have as much power over him.

Philippines

It is a much different ballgame. There, I hear no roaring chants from fans rooting for a touchdown, but deafening silence as people desire to receive the words of Jesus that I preach about. I see none of those eyes of adulation when we win games, but eyes of faith of people searching for Jesus who I talk about. You kind of find out from the get-go, what sets faith apart and what a game is just about.

—Filipinas *magazine, July 2009*

In Context

Tebow was born in Makati City, Philippines, on August 14, 1987. His parents were Christian missionaries to the Philippines and moved their entire family there for several years.

When he was fifteen years old and living in Florida, Tebow returned to the country of his birth, accompanying his father to the Philippines to do volunteer humanitarian work and preach the Gospel with the Bob Tebow Evangelistic Association.

When he's there, Tebow speaks at schools, visits hospitals and prisons, and helps put on medical clinics. He once performed circumcisions on poor children.

It's in the Philippines where Tebow developed his passion for ministering to orphans, as he spent time with the children at Uncle Dick's Home, the orphanage run by his father's ministry.

PREACHING

Great. It's special. When I do it, I feel like I can do it with so much passion and enjoyment and boldness, because I know how much it's changed my life and gave me peace and passion and purpose for life.

—GQ, *September 2009*

In Context

Tebow explained what it feels like when he preaches the Gospel of Jesus Christ. He derives much pleasure from offering the lasting joy he experiences as a believer to others.

Tebow believes the Gospel is the ultimate good news, and thus he preaches with passion and boldness. He preaches in churches and prisons in America, and in schools and other venues in the Philippines.

Preparation

*Honestly, I'm more sore from the workout I had
(Tuesday) than I am from the game.*

—The Denver Post *online, December 1, 2011*

In Context

Tebow made this statement after having run the ball
twenty-two times in a 16–13 overtime victory against the
San Diego Chargers, setting a record for most carries by a
quarterback in a single NFL game.

When questioned by reporters on how he felt after
getting hit and tackled so often during that game, Tebow
said that one of his recent workouts was more intense
and left him more sore than anything he experienced in
the game.

Tebow's workouts are brutal, and he pushes himself
hard and goes fast when doing them so that he can take
hits throughout the game and still have as much strength
and energy as possible at the end of games.

PRESSURE

I've always enjoyed pressure . . . Before every time I get up and give a speech, before every practice, before every football game I play, I always get a little bit nervous, and that's something that excites me, and I think it's something that I play better when I have more on the line, and that's something that I've always tried to thrive on, and when that feeling goes away, that will probably be the time when I stop playing football.

—*Press conference introducing Tebow as a New York Jet, March 26, 2012*

In Context

In his first press conference as a New York Jet, Tebow said he didn't feel any pressure to play well in the Big Apple because of the media coverage accompanying his arrival, although he expected he would eventually.

One might think that Tebow is such a seasoned pro at public speaking and playing football that he wouldn't get nervous before a speech or game, but he admits that he "always" does.

However, he embraces it rather than shies away from it, and uses that nervousness to help him focus on what he has to do to succeed. The pressure and nervousness he feels are clear markers that what he's about to do matters to him, and thus it's worth fighting through the jitters and getting on with it.

Pride

Well, I think the number one thing for me is knowing that everything that we have is a gift from God, and it can be taken away at any moment. And it's to make the most of it, with the talents that God gave us, to make the most of it . . . Everything that I'm given, I want to make the most of it, and be able to represent my talents in a way that are pleasing and glorifying to God . . . If we get proud about it, if you get proud about your athletic ability, or anything else, it can be taken away in a split second with an injury or with a tragedy or something happening.

—*"Easter on the Hill" service, Georgetown, Texas,*
April 8, 2012

In Context

During an Easter service, Tebow gave insight into how he stays centered in the midst of success and fame.

His answer brings to mind Proverbs 16:18: "Pride

goes before destruction; and a haughty spirit before stumbling."

Tebow believes that whatever talents and successes we have are gifts from God, so for us to get prideful over our abilities and accomplishments is foolish; it can also set us up for a fall.

Besides, because we can lose those talents at any time due to an injury or a tragedy outside of our control, we should be grateful and make the most of those talents while we have them.

Tebow himself experienced a taste of this during his senior year of college. He sustained a concussion against Kentucky, which put him in the hospital and kept him from practicing with his teammates for two weeks. He says it was a humbling experience to be knocked out and then have nothing to do but rest for days on end, unable to simply fight through it, unsure when or if he would play football again.

Principles
Before Gain

So many people, they were saying . . . If you do this you're going to lose a lot of endorsements, you're going to lose this, you're going to lose that. And you know what? It came to pass. I told them I was doing this commercial and two people that had already offered me a pretty significant contract for endorsement deals, they pulled them. They said we can't be associated with that. I said thank you. That means I don't want to be associated with you.

—*"Don Meyer Evening of Excellence,"*
Lipscomb University, April 17, 2010

In Context

Shortly before the 2010 NFL draft, Tebow appeared in a pro-life ad for Focus on the Family that ran during the Super Bowl. The ad referenced his mother's decision not to have an abortion when she was pregnant with him, despite her doctors' recommendation that she do so for health reasons.

The ad features Tebow's mother explaining why Tebow is her "miracle baby," because he almost didn't make it into this world but is now a healthy and strong young man.

Even though the ad doesn't mention abortion or the pro-life cause, pro-choice groups criticized Tebow for participating in it—yes, they criticized him for appearing in an ad that briefly discusses the circumstances of his own birth.

Tebow knew that he risked losing endorsement deals over this "controversial" commercial, but he filmed it anyway. And he did lose a couple of contracts, but he prefers to put his principles before financial gain.

PRIORITIES

*For me, every day includes four things: God,
family, academics, and football, in that order.*

—Florida Baptist Witness *online, August 29, 2007*

In Context

As much as Tebow loves playing football and winning
games, how much more devoted must he be to God, if he
put football last and God first in his four daily priorities
as a college student?

Promise Speech

I just want to say one thing. To the fans and everybody in Gator Nation: I'm sorry. I'm extremely sorry. You know, we were hoping for an undefeated season. That was my goal, something Florida's never done here.

But I promise you one thing: A lot of good will come out of this. You have never seen any player in the entire country play as hard as I will play the rest of this season, and you'll never see someone push the rest of the team as hard as I will push everybody the rest of this season, and you'll never see a team play harder than we will the rest of this season. God bless.

—Postgame press conference, Florida Gators vs. Ole Miss Rebels, September 27, 2008

In Context

Tebow made this promise during the press conference following Florida's 31–30 upset loss to Ole Miss early in the 2008 season. Fighting back tears because Florida's dream of an undefeated season was over, Tebow declared that he would work harder than any other player in the nation and that the Gators would work harder than any other team from that point forward for the rest of the season.

The Gators then went on to win all of their remaining games and the national championship.

Tebow's declaration became known as the "Promise Speech," and is now engraved on a plaque outside the front entrance to Florida's football facility.

PROVING
DOUBTERS WRONG

I did an interview the other day with someone on the NFL Network who said last year I'd never play a down in the NFL. He was wrong. Others who say I won't make it are wrong. They don't know what I'm capable of and what's inside me.

—The Denver Post *online, August 5, 2011*

In Context

During training camp before the 2011 NFL season, Tebow believed he was going to be the Denver Broncos' new starting quarterback. The Broncos were trying to trade starter Kyle Orton, and once he was gone, Tebow would step into his place as the starter.

At some point in camp, however, the trade fell through, and Denver decided to keep Orton as their starter. While these events were taking place, many football analysts were declaring Tebow to be a disaster. Merril Hoge, for example, said it was embarrassing to think Denver could win with Tebow and that Tebow could not make the necessary changes to become a good quarterback.

The quote from Tebow here came in the context of that entire situation, as he pushed back at his critics. He pointed out that he had already proven one huge doubt about his career wrong—that he would never play a down in the NFL—because the season before, Tebow started the Broncos' final three games.

PUBLIC
PROCLAMATION
OF FAITH

It's a great platform. When it's live, so they can't edit it, and I thank my Lord and Savior, Jesus Christ . . . I get to talk about this thing. I get to talk about my faith.

—*"For Such a Time as This" banquet,*
Stillwater Christian School, March 7, 2012

In Context

Tebow routinely begins interviews and press conferences, especially after games, by saying, "First and foremost, I just want to thank my Lord and Savior, Jesus Christ." He ends them by saying, "God bless."

Knowing how the media can edit his answers and statements during tapings before those appearances air, Tebow takes advantage of his live television interviews by praising God as the cameras roll.

PUSHING YOURSELF TO THE LIMIT

My dad set goals. Sometimes they were outrageous goals that some people wouldn't even think they could accomplish. But he believed in them and the people around him believed in him.

He would work as hard as he had to in order to get things done. He would work harder than people would believe you could work. When you have someone who believes [in] you and you believe in yourself you can accomplish so much more than you think you could accomplish. What I try to do with my focus and work ethic is to find out how hard I can push myself and then keep going.

—*"Don Meyer Evening of Excellence,"*
Lipscomb University, April 17, 2010

In Context

Tebow's father, Bob, is a pastor, missionary, and the founder of the Bob Tebow Evangelistic Association, which focuses on evangelism, church planting, training new missionaries, and running an orphanage in the Philippines.

As a boy, Tebow observed his father's "outrageous goals" and tenacious work ethic, and he has followed in those footsteps, by pushing himself as hard as he can in the pursuit of his goals.

Putting in Extra Work

I throw a lot. I do. I don't know, it depends on the day, I mean stuff like that I just stay out extra to work on little things, or practice, or ball placement, or just little things and I mean, that's also, just doing that, I love throwing, I love playing football. I know it looks like it could be extra work, it really is extra work, but it's also just having fun and just playing the game I love to play, so I would do that if I was at home, I'd go outside with my dad to throw.

—*"Denver Broncos Training Camp Quotes,"*
August 10, 2011

In Context

Tebow's work ethic is renowned, and he will put in the work necessary to improve in areas where he is weak.

Football analysts have long criticized Tebow's lengthy throwing motion, saying that it increases his odds of fumbling because defenders have more time to knock the ball out of his hand.

Tebow spent a lot of time in the months after his college career ended working on shortening his throwing motion in order to improve his NFL draft prospects. His improvement helped him get selected in the first round.

REACTION TO
BEING MOCKED

✦

Obviously, you don't know somebody's intentions, so I won't judge what he did. He was probably just having fun and was excited he made a good play and had a sack. And good for him. He was just celebrating and having fun with his teammates, and I don't take offense at that. I was more bothered I gave up the sack and didn't break the tackle.

—New York Post *online, November 3, 2011*

In Context

In a 45–10 loss to the Detroit Lions, Detroit linebacker Stephen Tulloch "Tebowed" next to Tebow after sacking him. When Tebow was asked if he took offense, he said no, assuming the best of intentions—that Tulloch "was just celebrating and having fun"—and then said that getting sacked was what really bothered him.

It's a classy, smart response from Tebow (even if he was actually biting his tongue), because publicly taking offense and getting in a war of words over the slight would only make him look petty.

Besides, if you're going to be so public in expressing your faith as Tebow is, then a certain amount of ridicule will necessarily come your way. It's part of the deal.

Tebow understands that, and he took the mocking in stride, and thus it never became a huge story.

Redeeming the Time

When you die, there's gonna be a tombstone, and on that tombstone there's gonna be a name, and there's gonna be a date. And for me, it's going to be 1987, and then it's gonna have a dash . . . I want that dash to mean something. I want that dash to be special. I want that dash to represent that Tim Tebow finished strong. And most importantly, when I get to heaven, I want Jesus to say, well done, my good and faithful servant.

—*"Night of Champions," Fellowship of Christian Athletes, May 2009*

In Context

Tebow is committed to living a life of significance that will resonate for all eternity. He has a sense of divine calling: His parents call him their "miracle baby" because he was born healthy despite his mother's health complications that led their doctors to recommend abortion; as a boy, Tebow's father told him that with his athletic ability, he would one day have a public platform to preach the Gospel.

Not everyone has that background of course, but Tebow encourages his listeners to make their lives count, both now and in heaven. We have all been given one chance at life on this earth and we will all die (unless Christ returns first), and thus Tebow's tombstone dash imagery (the dash representing the years we lived) is haunting.

But also motivating, because as long we're still alive, we can try to live meaningfully and finish strong, so that we will not come to the end of our lives with regret over having not pursued our dreams or having not lived righteously.

Self-Discipline

Love ice cream. I let myself have that about once a week. Vanilla.

—USA TODAY *online, January 12, 2012*

In Context

Tebow has loved ice cream since he was a boy.

But, to be as successful on the football field as he wants, Tebow knows he has to be in the best physical shape possible. Proper nutrition is a vital component to staying in top shape.

As much as Tebow loves vanilla ice cream, he disciplines himself to only enjoy it about once a week.

Many of us just eat whatever we want whenever we want, concerning ourselves only with how the food tastes, how convenient it is to access, or how much it costs. Whether or not the food is healthy is often of little to no consideration.

With two-thirds of American adults either overweight or obese, more of us would be wise to discipline ourselves in what we eat, by limiting our intake of fast food and sugary treats, as Tebow does.

Sexual Purity

Yes, I am. I think y'all are stunned right now.
You can't even ask me a question. First time ever.
Wow . . . I was ready for that question, I don't
think y'all were.

—*2009 SEC Media Days, July 23, 2009*

In Context

When Tebow was twenty-one years old, he was asked by a reporter if he was waiting for marriage before becoming sexually active.

Tebow answered that, yes, he was, and the idea that the nation's most famous college football player was sexually abstinent discombobulated the reporter as he tried to ask a follow-up question, causing the entire room to erupt in laughter.

For Tebow, the Bible is clear that sexual activity is for marriage. While everyone else makes a bigger deal out of his virginity than he does (it's not something he talks about unless asked), he viewed his answer to this question as an opportunity to encourage other young people to follow his example.

Sharing the Credit

Probably the pass because I can get one more player involved in the game. As long as we get a W, I don't care how it happens.

—*ESPN.com (Associated Press), February 2, 2012*

In Context

Tebow was asked whether he would prefer to run or pass if he had only one play to win a game.

If given a choice, he prefers to have a teammate share in the credit for the game-winning score, but ultimately, he just wants to win, however that happens.

Sources of
Inspiration

※

Quote books. I like to read quotes that are motivational. I stole a quote book from the [University of Florida] strength-and-conditioning coach. He kept asking when I was going to give it back.

—The Denver Post *online, December 17, 2011*

In Context

Tebow's relationship with Christ is his primary motivation and his parents are his two biggest sources of inspiration.

He is extremely self-motivated as well.

Another source of inspiration for Tebow are books with motivational quotes. Two quotes he mentions often in interviews are "Hard work beats talent when talent doesn't work hard," and "I don't know what the future holds, but I know Who holds my future."

Spreading the Gospel

Sometimes, you wonder that if I gave myself more free time, maybe I'd come back fresher and more rejuvenated [for football]. But at the same time, you don't want to miss out on the chance to impact people's lives. All these opportunities to spread God's message, you're not going to have them your whole life. So I want to push the limit. It can definitely wear you down, but I get so much joy from it that it picks me up.

—The Florida Times-Union *online, July 3, 2008*

In Context

Tebow's numerous speaking engagements, media interviews, and works of charity (such as visiting sick children or prisoners) are all ways for him to spread God's message.

He recognizes that our time on earth is brief, and he wants to "push the limit," to do as much as he can for the Lord before his time is up, even if it means he has a lot less time to relax and refresh.

STANDING OUT FROM THE CROWD

When you do things different than other people sometimes do them, and you don't settle for just being average, you open yourself up [for criticism]. But I'm ready for it. I've learned to live with it. I never just wanted to do things the same way everybody else does.

—*ESPN.com, April 22, 2010*

In Context

Tebow plays quarterback differently than the prototypical quarterback does, by running often and embracing hard contact with defenders; he lives differently than the average person does, by being open about his faith in God and holding himself to rigorous moral standards.

For both of these things, Tebow gets criticized. A lot.

But, he recognizes that comes with the territory: Refusing to be average (or "normal") often arouses resentment in those who prefer the typical way of doing things, especially if they're not willing to make the same sacrifices. A person who upholds a high moral code of personal conduct (even if they're humble and not self-righteous) can engender feelings of inadequacy in others, which can evince itself as hostility.

Tebow, however, has always embraced the idea of standing out in a positive way, and he doesn't let the negative opinions of others deter him from that course.

STANDING UP FOR
BELIEFS

*That's always going to be a part of who I am,
and I won't try to hide it. A team that doesn't
want that shouldn't take me. Pro-life is very
important to me. My mother listened to God late
in her pregnancy, and if she had listened to
others and terminated me, obviously I wouldn't
be here. If others don't have the same belief, it's
OK. I understand. But I hope they respect that at
least I have the courage to stand up for what I
believe in.*

—Sports Illustrated *online, "Monday Morning
Quarterback" column, January 25, 2010*

In Context

Tebow was asked if he thought doing a pro-life Super
Bowl commercial for Focus on the Family would hurt his
NFL draft prospects due to the controversy it caused.

He responded that if it did, he's fine with that, because he won't shy away from standing up for his beliefs, which in this case is the pro-life cause.

Considering that he wouldn't be here if his parents didn't believe that all life is valuable and a gift from God, his participation in the commercial makes perfect sense.

STAYING GROUNDED

My parents made sure I always understood that being good at something doesn't make you better than anyone else. I can play football, but anyone I meet can do something better than me.

—The Florida Times-Union *online, August 21, 2005*

In Context

Tebow's parents were committed to keeping him humble, a task no doubt made challenging because of his numerous athletic achievements and the massive media coverage that came with it.

As he began his senior year of high school and his popularity continued to grow, Tebow spoke about how he stays grounded, by keeping in mind a simple reality—that no matter how good any of us are at some particular thing, anyone we meet can do *something* better than us.

Keeping that insight in mind is a great way of holding our ego in check, no matter how successful we are in our chosen fields.

STRENGTHENING FAITH

‡

And for me as a Christian trying to grow closer to the Lord and continuing to try to strengthen my faith, one way you strengthen your faith is through obstacles, through adversity and there's definitely been some of that. Then, also something that strengthens your faith is when you have things go good, how you handle it. I think for me one of my biggest prayers is win or lose, good or bad, is that I'm the same guy, I honor the Lord either way and I treat people the exact same and I'm not changing no matter what happens.

—*Boston.com, December 14, 2011*

In Context

Tebow points out that it's not just when things go bad that we can strengthen our faith, but also when things are going well.

In times of plenty and success, we can get prideful or

feel less dependent on God; thus, when things are going well for us, it is also an opportunity to strengthen faith by asking for, and working to develop, humility.

Tebow carries himself with class and humility in interviews whether he has just won or just lost the game.

Studying

Most every Sunday, if my dad is not speaking,
I'll be in [the film room] from 12 to 8 or 9 at night.
Not because I have to be or they make me,
because I want to be here. I just spend all day
and I enjoy it. I enjoy coming here. Spending
time and learning. Also, it's a lot of fun doing it.
You learn a lot more. But also everyone else on
the team knows you're in here and they know
that you're working and preparing. It also gives
you that leadership aspect. If everyone knows
[you're] working the whole time, it gives you a
little more of a leadership role.

—The Quad: The New York Times College Sports Blog,
October 30, 2008

In Context

In college, Tebow voluntarily spent many hours in the film room studying game film, looking for insights to improve his play.

Many college athletes might prefer to relax on the

limited occasions when they have downtime, but Tebow wants to keep working, keep trying to improve.

As he says, it's also part of leadership. If the rest of the team sees him putting in extra work, it enhances his credibility when he pushes everyone else to work harder.

When Tebow played in the 2010 Senior Bowl (an exhibition showcasing top NFL draft prospects who have completed their senior year of college football), his coach was Tony Sparano, then the head coach of the Miami Dolphins. Sparano is a proponent of the Wildcat offense, which is distinguished by a direct snap to the running back, who can then hand off, run, or throw the ball, based on how the defense is set up.

Two years later, the New York Jets traded for Tebow to be their backup quarterback and signed Sparano to be their offensive coordinator. The Jets said they planned to regularly use Tebow in the Wildcat. Tebow told reporters he had kept Sparano's playbook from the Senior Bowl and was studying it in the weeks leading up to his first practices with his new team.

Supporting Teammates

That kind of irritated me. I really told Coach to just give me the ball, because I wanted to hit somebody extremely hard.

—Sports Illustrated *online, Inside College Football column, November 29, 2008*

In Context

In a 45–15 victory over the Florida State Seminoles, Seminole fans cheered as Florida wide receiver Percy Harvin left the game due to a sprained right ankle.

Two plays later, Tebow barreled through several Seminole defenders into the end zone for a 4-yard rushing touchdown, likely hitting more than one person extremely hard.

Tact

Well, I think for everybody that puts on a uniform, you want to go out there and you want to play. That's why you play the game of football. And I'm excited to be a Jet, to go out there and to help this team any way that I can. And whatever my role is, however I can expand that role, I'm going to try to do that. And every day in practice I'm going to go out there and compete and try to get better as a quarterback and try to figure out any ways possible to help this team any way that I can.

—*Press conference introducing Tebow as a New York Jet, March 26, 2012*

In Context

At the press conference introducing him to the New York media, Tebow answered a potentially dangerous question with tact and diplomacy.

He was asked if he hopes to be the Jets' starting quarterback even though Jets management made it clear from the moment they traded for him that he would be the backup to starter Mark Sanchez.

He didn't give a direct yes or no answer. If he said yes, then the media would immediately run stories saying that there's a "quarterback controversy" and that "Tebow is at odds with Jets management."

If he said no, then he would look weak and lacking in competitive fire and the media could run stories about how "Tebow resigns himself to being benchwarmer."

Instead, Tebow simply pointed out that every football player wants to be on the field playing, and then added that he will try to "expand" his role and that in practice he will "go out there and compete."

So, yes, Tebow wants to be the starter. But rather than talking about it in the media, he's focused on earning that job in practice and in games.

TEBOW TIME

That's when you have to get it done. Honestly,
that's why you lift, why you do everything as
much as you do. It's for the fourth quarter.
That's when it comes down to. You want to have
an opportunity in the fourth quarter to win
the game.

—*"Denver Broncos News Release: Denver Broncos*
Quotes," November 23, 2011

In Context

In the 2011 NFL season, Tebow led the Denver Broncos to five fourth-quarter comeback victories.

Broadcast announcers started saying "It's Tebow Time," when, late in the game and behind in the score, Tebow would begin a drive in pursuit of a comeback.

Tebow's workouts are intense and fast—he's constantly moving—and he does that so that his body will still be strong and energetic in the fourth quarter. This puts him in a better position to be able to pull out a late victory.

"Tebowing"

One of the reasons I get on a knee is because that's a form of humbling yourself. I want to humble myself before the Lord and say thank you for this opportunity. Thank you for letting me play the game I love. Whether I'm good or bad, whether I'm the hero or the goat, whether I score four touchdowns or throw four interceptions, that [I] will still be the same person, honoring the Lord.

—*Canyon Ridge Christian Church, Las Vegas, Nevada,
March 3, 2012*

In Context

Some observers think Tebow is grandstanding when he takes a knee to pray in the end zone before games or after touchdowns ("Tebowing"). They accuse Tebow of making it appear as though he has unique access to God's ear and favor, saying that he's asking God to grant him victory. He may well be praying for victory—we can't possibly know.

However, Tebow says he prays for the ability to remain humble and gracious whether he wins or loses. And he is adamant that his primary purpose in "Tebowing" is simply to humble himself before God in a public place so that he can demonstrate gratitude to God for the opportunity to play the game he loves.

Praying just before the game is also part of his pregame routine because it helps him control his emotions and stay focused on the task ahead.

Temptation

I think the number one way that you handle that is obviously by having a strong faith and relying on that and staying in the Word, but also by having a great support staff around you. By having friends that keep you accountable, by having just everyone in my family to having everyone that's involved, my agents, everything, to getting all that support staff that believe in me and also going to keep me accountable and make sure I'm doing the right thing.

—Hannity, *Fox News Channel, May 31, 2011*

In Context

Tebow's primary tool in resisting the myriad temptations that come with being a famous athlete is by relying on his faith in God and regularly reading the Bible.

But, recognizing that no man is an island and that he needs help, Tebow relies on a strong support staff. He looks to his family and friends, and others on his business team to hold him accountable and help him stay on the right track.

TIM TEBOW FOUNDATION

*My foundation is something that is extremely
important to me, and it's something that I'm very
proud of. And I'm so proud of the six hundred
and fifty orphans that we support, or the
eighteen Timmy's playrooms [in children's
hospitals throughout the world] that we're
building, or the hospital in the Philippines that
we're building, because ultimately I know that
that's more important than anything I do on the
football field, is the ability to brighten a kid's
day, or the ability to make someone smile.*

—Press conference introducing Tebow as a
New York Jet, March 26, 2012

In Context

Tebow founded his charity organization, the Tim Tebow
Foundation, in January 2010—as soon as he finished college. He would have done it earlier, but NCAA rules pro-
hibited it.

Tebow's goal with his foundation is to spread the Gospel of Jesus Christ and bring hope and healing to suffering people, children in particular.

The foundation has four primary outreaches:

- The W15H Program: affords sick children the opportunity to meet Tebow.
- CURE International Partnership: The first joint project is construction of a children's hospital in Davao City, Philippines. Focusing primarily on orthopedics, the hospital is expected to open in mid-2013.
- Timmy's Playrooms: creation of playrooms in children's hospitals throughout the world.
- Uncle Dick's Home: financial support for the orphanage in the Philippines run by his father's ministry, the Bob Tebow Evangelistic Association.

Tebow intends to devote himself full-time to the foundation once his professional football career ends.

Toughness

It's unfortunate, but a lot of people do think Christians have to be soft. But the man we are following is the toughest of all time in Jesus Christ. You have to go through obstacles and adversity. That's what provides endurance for the future.

God has everything in his hands but he also says, "Do unto the Lord with all your heart." Just because you are a Christian, God doesn't want you . . . not be the hardest worker. It's just the opposite. He wants you to work harder.

—Yahoo! Sports, *December 14, 2011*

In Context

Tebow notes that a popular misconception is that Christians have to be soft.

The truth, however, is that Jesus Christ Himself "is the toughest [man] of all time," as Tebow says.

Jesus fasted for forty days and forty nights alone in the wilderness, fending off temptation by the devil.

Jesus used a whip to drive out the money changers from the temple and overturned their tables, yelling at them to stop making God's house a house of trade.

Jesus suffered crucifixion. He was flogged, crowned with thorns, beaten, and forced to carry His own cross. He was then nailed to the cross by His hands and feet.

Three days later, He rose from the dead.

That's as tough as it gets.

TRASH TALKING

I don't think it's ever really a good thing to talk trash because all it does is fire your opponent up. At least that's how it is for me.

—The Independent Florida Alligator *online,*
October 8, 2008

In Context

Tebow himself doesn't talk trash, but he once had a memorable response to an opponent who was giving it to him hard.

In Florida's 24–14 victory over Oklahoma in the 2009 BCS National Championship game, Tebow picked up what may be the only unsportsmanlike conduct penalty of his entire football career, at any level.

Oklahoma player Nic Harris got in Tebow's face after tackling him and trash-talked, and as Tebow walked backwards, he clapped his hands in the motion of an alligator chomping down on its prey—the "Gator Chomp."

Tebow was flagged for an unsportsmanlike conduct penalty, but it had no bearing on the outcome of the game.

TRUE SATISFACTION

I found true satisfaction, true happiness, and it is not by having your name in a newspaper, it is not by winning trophies, it is not by winning championships, it is by having a relationship with Jesus Christ.

—Beyond the Ultimate *website*

In Context

Tebow's comment on where he has found true satisfaction is reminiscent of Mark 8:36: "For what does it profit a man to gain the whole world, and forfeit his soul?"

All of Tebow's success on the football field—setting records, winning championships—doesn't satisfy his soul nearly as much as does his relationship with Jesus Christ.

TRUSTING GOD

⊹

The way I figure is if nothing bad ever happened,
there wouldn't be a need for faith. The Bible says
we're tested and made stronger through trials
and tribulations. But He's here, helping us
out . . . God has a plan for everything.

—ESPN The Magazine, *September 21, 2009*

In Context

Tebow's thoughts on trusting God call to mind 1 Peter 1:
6–7: "In this you greatly rejoice, even though now for a
little while, if necessary, you have been distressed by various trials, so that the proof of your faith, being more
precious than gold which is perishable, even though
tested by fire, may be found to result in praise and glory
and honor at the revelation of Jesus Christ."

While Tebow's mother was pregnant with him, her
and her husband's faith was tested through various trials: Pam Tebow suffered so much pain and bleeding leading up to the birth that their doctors recommended
abortion to save her life. Not only that, but many times

during the pregnancy, the Tebows thought their son had been miscarried.

But believing that all children deserve a chance at life, that abortion is sinful, and that God has a plan for everything, the Tebows trusted God and proceeded with the pregnancy.

Ultimately, Tim Tebow was born healthy, grew to be strong and athletic, and now takes God's message to the masses through the fame his football exploits grant him.

Victory

Oh, man, ya'll have a lot of different statistics . . .
It's about wins and losses.

—The Gazette *online, December 15, 2011*

In Context

Tebow made the above comment to reporters who questioned him about his sometimes poor passing statistics.

His unorthodox quarterbacking style and tepid passing numbers have been criticized constantly, and his detractors point to those two things as evidence that Tebow should not be a starting quarterback in the NFL.

But, what ultimately matters in sports?

Winning games.

And that's what Tebow did in his first year as the Denver Broncos starter, taking the team from a 1–4 record and in last place in their division, to an 8–8 record, first place in their division, and to a victory in the first round of the playoffs.

Winning ugly trumps losing pretty every time.

Tebow wants to win—how he wins is far less important to him.

Visiting Prisoners

You're talking to guys who don't have much to look forward to in life there. They made some bad decisions and they're in there. A lot don't have much hope or anything to look at as positive . . . I just try and give them hope that there is something good and something to look forward to. They need to know that just because they're in prison, their life still means something.

—The Quad: The New York Times College Sports Blog,
September 12, 2007

In Context

Tebow has said visiting prisoners and sharing the Gospel with them is one of his favorite things to do. He began doing it early in his college career.

He says that while many of the hard-edged guys in prison won't pay much mind to a typical preacher, they will listen to Tim Tebow. In fact, he says his style of play (hard running, never backing down, full contact with defenders) resonates with many prisoners. His quarterbacking style is blue-collar and tough, like many of them.

In this quote, he's talking about having met with men who are in prison for life, some of whom are murderers and drug lords. Many people simply do not have compassion or concern for such men, but Tebow's heart extends even to them. He wants to spend time with them and see them come to know the Lord.

Visiting
Suffering Fans

✦

It's by far the best thing I do to get myself ready. Here you are, about to play a game that the world says is the most important thing in the world. Win and they praise you. Lose and they crush you. And here I have a chance to talk to the coolest, most courageous people. It puts it all into perspective. The game doesn't really matter. I mean, I'll give one hundred percent of my heart to win it, but in the end, the thing I most want to do is not win championships or make a lot of money, it's to invest in people's lives, to make a difference.

—*ESPN.com, Rick Reilly column, January 13, 2012*

In Context

As part of the Tim Tebow Foundation, the W15H program fulfills the wishes of people (usually children, but also adults) who are suffering from serious health problems and whose dream is to meet Tim Tebow.

W15H stands for the word "wish" with Tebow's jersey number, 15, standing in for the "is" in "wish." The Tim Tebow Foundation partners with Dreams Come True, a Jacksonville-based wish granting organization, to accomplish this.

It is a year-round effort, but during the NFL season, Tebow arranges to bring a suffering fan and his or her family to each game that he plays, both home and away. Their transportation, hotel, meals, and game tickets are paid for by the foundation. Tebow meets with the fan before the game, and sometimes after it as well.

What the
Future Holds

━┿━

You know? I'm not sure. I don't know what the future holds, but I know Who holds my future. And that's something that has always given me peace and comfort. And that's why I don't have to worry about the future. I can just worry about today and worry about becoming better as a football player, as a person, and trying to improve, and just living one day at a time.

—The Michael Kay Show, *March 30, 2012*

In Context

Tebow was asked if he thought that he would be a starting quarterback in the NFL again, after having gone from being the starter for the Denver Broncos to the backup for the New York Jets. His answer? He honestly doesn't know.

He will certainly work as hard as he can to make that happen, but he knows he doesn't control the future. God does.

James 4:14 says, "Yet you do not know what your life will be like tomorrow. You are just a vapor that appears for a little while and then vanishes away."

Because Tebow recognizes that we don't know what the future holds, but we do know Who is in charge of the future, we can set aside worry about the future and instead spend our time and energy making the most of the present.

Influential Scriptures

‡

Tebow often refers to passages from the Bible in interviews, press conferences, speeches, and other public statements. He wore Bible verses on his eye black during the last two seasons of his college football career.

This is a compilation of ten Scriptures that Tebow references frequently and has acknowledged as being highly influential in his approach to life.

Note: All Scriptures are from the New American Standard Bible.

Proverbs 27:2

> *"Let another praise you, and not your own mouth;*
> *A stranger, and not your own lips."*

When Tebow was a boy, his parents instituted a "humility rule" for him and his two brothers, as they each began to have significant athletic success: They were not allowed to talk about their accomplishments unless first asked about them by someone else. Tebow has said that the rule was based on Proverbs 27:2. Today, despite enormous acclaim, Tebow remains humble, praising God first, his teammates and coaches second, while minimizing talk about himself, except in response to direct questions.

Matthew 28:19–20

"Go therefore and make disciples of all the nations, baptizing them in the name of the Father and the Son and the Holy Spirit, teaching them to observe all that I commanded you; and lo, I am with you always, even to the end of the age."

In his autobiography, Tebow explains that Matthew 28:19–20 is a guiding verse for his family, informing their entire way of life. As Christian missionaries, Bob Tebow and his wife, Pam, instilled in their children a passion for spreading the Gospel, and Tebow's enthusiasm for speaking about Jesus continues to this day.

Luke 12:48b

"From everyone who has been given much, much will be required; and to whom they entrusted much, of him they will ask all the more."

Tebow feels a responsibility to use the gifts God has given him as well as he possibly can, and a burden not to waste them. He views doing so as a means of thanking

God for his abilities. For him, that means playing as hard and as well as he can on the football field. It also means using the public platform that football affords him to both speak about Jesus and minister to the physical and emotional needs of suffering children around the world.

John 3:16

> *"For God so loved the world, that He gave His only*
> *begotten Son, that whoever believes in Him shall*
> *not perish, but have eternal life."*

In the Florida Gators' 24–14 victory over the Oklahoma Sooners in the 2009 BCS National Championship game, Tebow wore John 3:16 on his eye black.

During the game and the day after, John 3:16 was the top search phrase on Google, garnering more than 90 million searches.

This verse is the essence of the Christian Gospel.

Romans 1:16

> *"For I am not ashamed of the gospel, for it is the*
> *power of God for salvation to everyone who*
> *believes, to the Jew first and also to the Greek."*

Tebow is clear that he is never ashamed or afraid of proclaiming his faith in Jesus Christ, often in very public ways. He believes that the Gospel is good news for everyone who hears him speak about it. He wore Romans 1:16 on his eye black in 2009 against Florida International.

Ephesians 4:32

> *"Be kind to one another, tender-hearted, forgiving*
> *each other, just as God in Christ also has*
> *forgiven you."*

Tebow tries to be kind and gracious to everyone he meets, and it is evident in almost every interview he gives. He is more concerned with the work of his charity foundation than he is about his success in football. Tebow doesn't lash out at his many critics or even really respond to them. When he's asked about them, he tends to say something nice about them before addressing the criticism. He wore Ephesians 4:32 on his eye black in 2009 against Mississippi State.

Philippians 4:13

> *"I can do all things through Him*
> *who strengthens me."*

The first time Tebow wore a Scripture on his eye black, he chose Philippians 4:13, a verse he says encapsulates his approach to football. He wore this verse on his eye black throughout the 2008 regular season.

Colossians 3:23

> *"Whatever you do, do your work heartily,*
> *as for the Lord rather than for men."*

Tebow has said many times that he believes in going hard in everything he does, and putting his all into it, no matter what the task before him is. His intense work ethic is lauded even by his critics. He wore Colossians 3:23 on his eye black against Vanderbilt in 2009.

2 Timothy 4:7

> *"I have fought the good fight, I have finished*
> *the course, I have kept the faith."*

Tebow often speaks on the importance of both never quitting and also finishing strong, in whatever task is before him. He has said that he never quit anything that he started, and that is the key to achieving his goals. More than that, however, Tebow has also said his ultimate goal in life is to enter heaven and be embraced by Jesus, as the Lord tells him that he finished strong in his pursuit to glorify God on earth.

James 1:2–4

> *"Consider it all joy, my brethren, when you*
> *encounter various trials, knowing that the*
> *testing of your faith produces endurance. And*
> *let endurance have its perfect result, so that you*
> *may be perfect and complete, lacking in nothing."*

Tebow wore James 1:2–4 on his eye black during the Senior Bowl, where top NFL draft prospects showcase their talents. Tebow later explained that he chose that passage for the game to signify his resolve in the face of the torrent of criticism he faced from football analysts regarding his quarterbacking skills.

ACKNOWLEDGMENTS

Thank you to:

George and Mary Beahm, my uncle and aunt, for believing in this project from the get-go. George, your help on the proposal and guidance throughout the writing process was crucial to this book's existence.

Scott Mendel, my agent, to whom George introduced me. Scott, your confidence in this book and high level of professionalism have been extremely helpful.

Joel Fotinos, publisher at Tarcher, for taking such a strong interest in this book and being determined to see it published despite several obstacles along the way.

Andrew Yackira, my editor at Tarcher, for your input, encouragement, and willingness to help whenever needed.

Phillip Hines, my younger brother, for your honest critiques of the book, which made the focus and content sharper, and for helping with fact-checking and proofing.

Luke Hines, my youngest brother, for your assistance in fact-checking and proofing.

SOURCES

EPIGRAPH

Ellsworth, Tim. "Tebow: Standing Alone a Key to Significance." *Baptist Press*. April 20, 2010. http://www.bpnews.net/bpnews.asp?id=32751

Action
Workman, Jim. "Tebow Asks Listeners to Impact Others' Lives." *Bluefield Daily Telegraph* online. January 31, 2010. http://bdtonline.com/localsports/x1071713546/Tebow-asks-listeners-to-impact-others-lives

Adaptability
"Denver Broncos Training Camp Quotes." Denver Broncos News Release. August 10, 2011. http://media.denverbroncos.com/images/9008/Transcripts/110810_Tebow.pdf

Anxiety
"Tebow Introduced by Jets." NFL.com. Video of Tebow press conference. Transcribed from video. Uploaded on March 26, 2012. http://www.nfl.com/videos/new-york-jets/09000d5d827df421/Tebow-introduced-by-Jets

Attitude
Schonbrun, Zach. "Tebow Draws Crowd as Jets Open Locker Room." *The New York Times* online. May 10, 2012. http://www.nytimes.com/2012/05/11/sports/football/tim-tebow-draws-crowd-as-jets-open-locker-room.html

Being a Role Model
Serby, Steve. "Serby's Exclusive Q&A with . . . Tim Tebow." *New York Post* online. December 15, 2011. http://www.nypost.com/p/sports/more_sports/serby_exclusive_with_tim_tebow_umO1GNRjsz53WWbzbQTZMN/0

Belief

Hubbuch, Bart. "Tebow Fever Still Growing." *New York Post* online. December 13, 2011. http://www.nypost.com/p/sports/more_sports/ tim_to_believe_2TihhboFBk5rj7S62PnJKL

Biblical Role Models

Frenette, Gene. "No Down Time for Tebow, Who's Up for His Mission." *The Florida Times-Union* online (Jacksonville.com). July 3, 2008. http://jacksonville.com/tu-online/stories/070308/spf_299150840 .shtml

Brightening Someone's Day

English, Antonya. "Tebow Makes a Fan's Day." *Tampa Bay Times*. December 11, 2009. http://www.tampabay.com/sports/college/ article1058014.ece

Character Formation

"Timeout with Tebow: Video Series 4 of 6." YouTube video. Transcribed from video. Uploaded by Jockey on December 26, 2011. http://www .youtube.com/watch?v=Xsk0fSj3RYk&feature=relmfu

Compassion

"Tim Tebow Announces the Tebow CURE Hospital." CURE International website. Video of announcement. Transcribed from video. http:// cure.org/my/tebow/

Competitiveness

Cimini, Rich. "Notes: Tebow Will Do 'Whatever It Takes.'" ESPNNewYork .com, New York Jets blog. May 26, 2012. http://espn.go.com/blog/ new-york/jets/post/_/id/12641/notes-tebow-will-do-whatever-it- takes

Contentment

McBrayer, Brad. "Tim Tebow: (Super) Man of Faith." *Baptist Press*. September 21, 2009. http://www.bpsports.net/bpsports.asp?ID= 6093

Controlling Emotions

"Denver Broncos Training Camp Quotes." August 12, 2010. http://media .denverbroncos.com/images/9008/Transcripts/100812_Tebow.pdf

Dealing with Critics

Stephens, Mitch. "Tim Tebow Draws from High School Days at Nease." MaxPreps.com. February 16, 2010. http://www.maxpreps.com/ news/AmVWLhtREd-UswAcxJTdpg/tim-tebow-draws-from-high- school-days-at-nease.htm

Decision-Making

Habib, Hal. "Tim Tebow an Unconventional Quarterback? He Can Find Some Role Models by Looking Back in NFL History." *The Palm Beach*

Post online. October 20, 2011. http://www.palmbeachpost.com/news/sports/football/tim-tebow-an-unconventional-quarterback-he-can-fin/nLy37/

Determination
"WINGED FOOT AWARD: Excerpts from Tim Tebow's Speech." *Naples Daily News* online. May 26, 2011. http://www.naplesnews.com/news/2011/may/26/winged-foot-award-excerpts-tim-tebows-speech/

Enjoying Life
Adams, Sam. "Tim Tebow: Dead Solid Perfect." *Colorado AvidGolfer* online. September 12, 2011. http://www.coloradoavidgolfer.com/golfers/tim-tebow-dead-solid-perfect.aspx

Expectations
"Denver Broncos News Release: Denver Broncos Quotes." October 11, 2011. http://media.denverbroncos.com/images/9008/Transcripts/111011_Tebow.pdf

Eye Black Scriptures
Lewis, Ted. "Tim Tebow's Eye Black Bible Verses: A Guide." *Times-Picayune* (al.com). December 29, 2009. http://blog.al.com/press-register-sports/2009/12/tim_tebows_eye_black_bible_ver.html

Faith
Stapleton, Arnie. "Tebow Mixes Faith and Football with No Apologies." Boston.com (Associated Press). December 14, 2011. http://articles.boston.com/2011-12-14/sports/30516880_1_tebow-coach-john-fox-teammates

Fighting Complacency
"Gators Speak At SEC Football Media Day." Gatorzone.com. July 23, 2009. http://www.gatorzone.com/story.php?id=16256

Finishing Strong
Workman, Jim. "Tebow Asks Listeners to Impact Others' Lives." *Bluefield Daily Telegraph* online. January 31, 2010. http://bdtonline.com/localsports/x1071713546/Tebow-asks-listeners-to-impact-others-lives

First Impressions
Hubbuch, Bart. "Tebow Ready for Jets Workouts." *New York Post* online. April 15, 2012. http://www.nypost.com/p/sports/jets/qb_set_for_crack_of_dawn_arrival_M6C9DK8TeKNH4gQ3hnvcJK

Fitness
"Tim Tebow's NFL Off-Season Workout." *Stack TV*. Transcribed from video. February 1, 2012. http://magazine.stack.com/TheIssue/Article/8494/the_secret_to_tim_tebows_success.aspx

Focus

Korfhage, Stuart. "Tracking Tebow." *St. Augustine Record* online. December 25, 2005. http://staugustine.com/stories/122505/spo_3535242.shtml

Football Role Model

Rogeberg, Tom. "Born To Lead." *Sharing the Victory*. August/September 2009. http://www.sharingthevictory.com/vsItemDisplay.lsp?method=display&objectid=C1DB34BF-C29A-EE7A-EA8321949419E6C3

Getting Back Up

Wine, Steven. "Tebow Rallies Broncos to Overtime Win Against Dolphins." *New York Post* online (Associated Press). October 24, 2011. http://www.nypost.com/p/sports/more_sports/better_believe_it_64dlIFo2ZMzqgLDsxxC09J

Giving God the Glory

"Tebow SLAMS Jake Plummer; Explains How God Helps Him." YouTube video of ESPN *First Take*. Transcribed from video. Uploaded by spac3wars on November 22, 2011. http://www.youtube.com/watch?v=P9oSpQprZ9I

God's Sovereignty

Schlabach, Mark. "Heisman Provides Tebow Broader Audience for Message of Faith." ESPN.com. May 5, 2008. http://sports.espn.go.com/ncf/columns/story?columnist=schlabach_mark&id=3381810

Going Hard

Smith, Guerry. "Competitive Fire Fuels Tebow." Gator Bait Magazine's *Florida Football 2007* preseason yearbook. 2007. http://virginiapreps.rivals.com/content.asp?CID=748732

Graciousness

@TimTebow. Twitter.com. Screenshot re-posting of tweet from March 29, 2012, which was hidden by pop-up survey. March 30, 2012. http://twitter.com/TimTebow/status/185723256471437314/photo/1

Handling Fame

Menez, Gene. "Talkin' with Tebow: Catching Up with Florida's Heisman Trophy Favorite." SI.com. December 7, 2007. http://sportsillustrated.cnn.com/2007/writers/gene_menez/12/06/tebow.interview/index.html

Hard Work

English, Antonya. "Former Florida Star Quarterback Tim Tebow Drafted in First Round by Denver Broncos." *Tampa Bay Times*. April 23, 2010. http://www.tampabay.com/sports/football/bucs/former-florida-star-quarterback-tim-tebow-drafted-in-first-round-by-denver/1089686

How to Improve America
"'Easter on the Hill,' Georgetown, TX, Tim Tebow." YouTube video of "Easter on the Hill" service. Transcribed from video. Uploaded by madmat1963 on April 8, 2012. http://www.youtube.com/watch?v=UZVeJYPBVFg

How to Succeed
"Tim Tebow's NFL Off-Season Workout." *Stack TV.* Transcribed from video. February 1, 2012. http://magazine.stack.com/TheIssue/Article/8494/the_secret_to_tim_tebows_success.aspx

Humility
Purks, Scott. "Everyone's All-American: Nease's Tim Tebow Is One of the Nation's Premier Prep QBs." *St. Petersburg Times* online (now *Tampa Bay Times*). December 9, 2005. http://www.sptimes.com/2005/12/09/news_pf/Sports/Everyone_s_All_Americ.shtml

Ignoring Distractions
"Face to Face: Tim Tebow." ESPN.com. Video clip of program. Transcribed from video. February 3, 2012. http://espn.go.com/video/clip?id=7537577

Influence
DiRocco, Michael. "Tim Tebow's Legacy: Away from Football, Gators Quarterback Focuses on Christian Faith, Charity, Mission Work." *The Florida Times-Union* (Jacksonville.com). November 27, 2009. Updated March 20, 2010. http://jacksonville.com/sports/college/florida_gators/2009-11-27/story/tim_tebows_legacy_away_from_football_gators_quarterba

Intangibles
Thamel, Pete. "The Quad Q&A: Tim Tebow." *The Quad: The New York Times College Sports Blog. New York Times* online. August 28, 2009. http://thequad.blogs.nytimes.com/2009/08/28/the-quad-qa-tim-tebow-2/#

Integrity
Frenette, Gene. "Q&A with Tim Tebow: On His Autobiography, Competing to Be a Starter and His Bachelor Status." *The Florida Times-Union* (Jacksonville.com). February 21, 2011. http://jacksonville.com/sports/college/florida-gators/2011-02-21/story/qa-tim-tebow-his-autobiography-competing-be-starter

Intensity
Fowler, Jeremy. "Make or Break: Florida QB Tim Tebow and Georgia QB Matt Stafford Fight to Establish Legacy in Heated Rivalry." *Orlando Sentinel* online. November 1, 2008. http://articles.orlandosentinel.com/2008-11-01/sports/fbcuf01_1_tim-tebow-stafford-gators

Jesus Christ

"'Easter on the Hill,' Georgetown, TX, Tim Tebow." YouTube video of "Easter on the Hill" service. Transcribed from video. Uploaded by madmat1963 on April 8, 2012. http://www.youtube.com/watch?v=UZVeJYPBVFg

Leadership

Whiteside, Kelly. "Florida's Tebow Hopes to Raise His Game, Looks for Third Title." *USA TODAY* online. July 28, 2009. http://www.usatoday.com/sports/college/football/2009-07-28-sw-florida-tebow_N.htm

Learning from Failure

"Denver Broncos News Release: Denver Broncos Quotes." December 28, 2011. http://media.denverbroncos.com/images/9008/Transcripts/111228_Tebow.pdf

Legacy

"Tim Tebow on 'Hannity.'" *Fox News* online. Video clip of *Hannity*. Transcribed from video. Uploaded on May 31, 2011. http://video.foxnews.com/v/969875443001/tim-tebow-on-hannity

Living by Faith

Bailey, Sarah Pulliam. "Q & A: Tim Tebow on Faith, Fame, & Football." *Christianity Today* magazine online. June 10, 2011. http://www.christianitytoday.com/ct/2011/juneweb-only/qatimtebow.html

Living in Light of Eternity

Richardson, Suzy. "A Gator for God." *Charisma* magazine online. September 30, 2008. http://www.charismamag.com/index.php/features/2008/october/17874-a-gator-for-god

Living with Passion

"Tim Tebow at Lipscomb University (04.17.2010) 3 of 4.wmv." YouTube video of "Don Meyer Evening of Excellence, Lipscomb University." Transcribed from video. Uploaded by PositiveRoleModels4U on April 28, 2010. http://www.youtube.com/watch?v=-JgjJWUMETY&context=C49c4037ADvjVQa1PpcFNlLBtEjJdH03qvKctSBH0bWkq1cQJx5ec=

Losing

Darlington, Jeff. "Tebow's Day Not Ruined by High-Profile Loss to Patriots." NFL.com. December 19, 2011. Updated December 20, 2011. http://www.nfl.com/news/story/09000d5d82533f7d/article/tebows-day-not-ruined-by-highprofile-loss-to-patriots

Making Sacrifices

Herchel, Mike. "Tim Tebow Interview from SEC Media Days." GatorTailgating.com. July 24, 2008. http://www.gatortailgating.com/content/tim-tebow-interview-sec-media-days

Modesty

Denman, Barbara. "Top Quarterback Recruit Aims to Stay Grounded in Christ." *Baptist Press*. January 24, 2006. http://www.bpnews.net/bpnews.asp?id=22513

Most Important Thing in Life

"Tebow Introduced by Jets." NFL.com. Video of Tebow press conference. Transcribed from video. Uploaded on March 26, 2012. http://www.nfl.com/videos/new-york-jets/09000d5d827df421/Tebow-introduced-by-Jets

Motivation

Rogeberg, Tom. "Born to Lead." *Sharing The Victory*. August/September 2009. http://www.sharingthevictory.com/vsItemDisplay.lsp?method=display&objectid=C1DB34BF-C29A-EE7A-EA8321949419E6C3

Moving Forward

"Michael Kay: 3/30." ESPNNewYork.com. Audio of radio interview. Transcribed from audio. March 30, 2012. http://espn.go.com/espnradio/newyork/play?id=7757176

Never Giving Up

Zaas, Stuart. "Broncos at Patriots: Quotables." *Denver Broncos Blog*. January 14, 2012. http://blog.denverbroncos.com/denverbroncos/broncos-at-patriots-quotables-2/

Nutrition

"Tim Tebow Trains for the NFL." *Stack TV*. YouTube video. Transcribed from video. Uploaded by STACKVids on June 8, 2010. http://www.youtube.com/watch?v=gVmXBa5HyI4

Orphans

Frenette, Gene. "Q&A with Tim Tebow: On His Autobiography, Competing to Be a Starter and His Bachelor Status." *The Florida Times-Union* online (Jacksonville.com). February 21, 2011. http://jacksonville.com/sports/college/florida-gators/2011-02-21/story/qa-tim-tebow-his-autobiography-competing-be-starter

Passion for Goals

"WINGED FOOT AWARD: Excerpts from Tim Tebow's Speech." *Naples Daily News* online. May 26, 2011. http://www.naplesnews.com/news/2011/may/26/winged-foot-award-excerpts-tim-tebows-speech/

Passion for the Gospel

Noah, Mickey. "Tebow: Football, NFL Not Source of True Success." *Baptist Press*. July 7, 2010. http://www.bpnews.net/bpnews.asp?ID=33293

Patience
Pasquarelli, Len. "The Wait Is Worth It for Tebow." ESPN.com. April 22, 2010. http://sports.espn.go.com/nfl/draft10/columns/story?columnist=pasquarelli_len&id=5127828

Perseverance
DiRocco, Michael. "Tim Tebow: Swamp King." *Men's Fitness*. September 2008. http://www.mensfitness.com/leisure/sports/tim-tebow-swamp-king

Perspective—It's Just a Game
Mayne, Kenny. "I Feel Like You Mocked My Question." *ESPN The Magazine*. September 21, 2009. http://insider.espn.go.com/ncf/insider/news/story?id=4455331

Philippines
Vicera, Nick. "The Philippines Is in His Heart." *Filipinas* magazine. July 2009. http://www.filipinasmag.com/?p=496#more-496

Preaching
Fagone, Jason. "Does God Have a Tim Tebow Complex?" *GQ*. September 2009. http://www.gq.com/sports/profiles/200908/tebow-florida-heisman-nfl-photos-quarterback-injury-concussion

Preparation
Klis, Mike. "Tim Tebow Loves to Run, and NFL Legend Billy Kilmer Right Behind Him." *The Denver Post* online. December 1, 2011. http://www.denverpost.com/broncos/ci_19445195

Pressure
"Tebow Introduced by Jets." NFL.com. Video of Tebow press conference. Transcribed from video. Uploaded on March 26, 2012. http://www.nfl.com/videos/new-york-jets/09000d5d827df421/Tebow-introduced-by-Jets

Pride
"'Easter on the Hill,' Georgetown, TX, Tim Tebow." YouTube video of Easter on the Hill service. Transcribed from video. Uploaded by madmat1963 on April 8, 2012. http://www.youtube.com/watch?v=UZVeJYPBVFg

Principles Before Gain
"Tim Tebow at Lipscomb University (04.17.2010) 2 of 4.wmv." YouTube video of "Don Meyer Evening of Excellence," Lipscomb University. Transcribed from video. Uploaded by PositiveRoleModels4U on April 28, 2010. http://www.youtube.com/watch?v=Sh5F5Lu_Bd0&feature=plcp

Priorities
Smith, Sr., James A. "Opponents on the Gridiron—Brothers in Christ."

Florida Baptist Witness online. August 29, 2007. http://www.gofbw
.com/News.asp?ID=7759

Promise Speech

"Tim Tebow's Promise and Pledge Become True." YouTube video of
Tebow's Promise Speech. Transcribed from video. Uploaded by
FireObsession on January 9, 2009. http://www.youtube.com/
watch?v=4sGv2Zw-WQw

Proving Doubters Wrong

Paige, Woody. "Broncos' Tim Tebow Dealing with Tension, Frustration."
The Denver Post online. August 5, 2011. http://www.denverpost.com/
paige/ci_18621060

Public Proclamation of Faith

Albertson, Kristi. "Tebow a Hit with Kalispell crowd." *The Daily Inter
Lake* online. March 7, 2012. Updated March 8, 2012. http://www
.dailyinterlake.com/news/local_montana/article_f24c0ea4-68e0-
11e1-b61b-001871e3ce6c.html?TNNoMobile

Pushing Yourself to the Limit

"Tebow Inspires Crowd at Meyer 'Evening of Excellence.'"
LipscombSports.com. April 17, 2010. http://www.lipscombsports
.com/news/archives-print/2009-10/5511/tebow-inspires-crowd-at-
meyer-evening-of-excellence/

Putting in Extra Work

"Denver Broncos News Release: Denver Broncos Training Camp Quotes."
August 10, 2011. http://media.denverbroncos.com/images/9008/
Transcripts/110810_Tebow.pdf

Reaction to Being Mocked

Hubbuch, Bart. "Broncos' Tebow Shrugs off Lions' Mocking." *New York
Post* online. November 3, 2011. http://www.nypost.com/p/sports/
more_sports/keeping_it_kneel_a4ZRY7ZG2MksybPaow0LDJ

Redeeming the Time

Fagone, Jason. "Does God Have a Tim Tebow Complex?" *GQ*. September
2009. http://www.gq.com/sports/profiles/200908/tebow-florida-
heisman-nfl-photos-quarterback-injury-concussion

Self-Discipline

Saraceno, Jon. "Tebow: The Man Behind the Mania." *USA TODAY* online.
January 12, 2012. Updated January 13, 2012. http://www.usatoday
.com/sports/football/nfl/story/2012-01-11/tebow-exclusive/525181
22/1?loc=interstitialskip

Sexual Purity

"Tim Tebow Is a Virgin." YouTube video of Tebow at SEC Media Days.
Transcribed from video. Uploaded by SanfordKnowsBest on July 23,

2009. http://www.youtube.com/watch?v=HS8qqNnR3aM&feature=
player_embedded

Sharing the Credit
"'Tebowmania' Comes to Super Bowl." ESPN.com (Associated Press).
February 2, 2012. http://sports.espn.go.com/espn/wire?section=
nfl&id=7532998

Sources of Inspiration
Paige, Woody. "Tebow Driven by Motivational Quotes—and Waiting for
You, Mr. Elway." *The Denver Post* online. December 17, 2011. http://
www.denverpost.com/paige/ci_19565637

Spreading the Gospel
Frenette, Gene. "No Down Time for Tebow, Who's Up for His Mission."
The Florida Times-Union (Jacksonville.com). July 3, 2008. http://
jacksonville.com/tu-online/stories/070308/spf_299150840.shtml

Standing Out from the Crowd
Pasquarelli, Len. "The Wait Is Worth It for Tebow." ESPN.com. April 22,
2010.   http://sports.espn.go.com/nfl/draft10/columns/story?
columnist=pasquarelli_len&id=5127828

Standing Up for Beliefs
King, Peter. "Monday Morning Quarterback." SI.com. January 25, 2010.
http://sportsillustrated.cnn.com/2010/writers/peter_king/01/24/
titlegames/2.html

Staying Grounded
Goodbread, Chase. "Everybody's All-American." *The Florida Times-
Union* (Jacksonville.com). August 21, 2005. http://jacksonville.com/
tu-online/stories/082105/hig_19557306.shtml

Strengthening Faith
Benbow, Julian. "All Tim Tebow, All the Time." Boston.com. December
14, 2011. http://articles.boston.com/2011-12-14/sports/30516961_1_
tim-tebow-faith-press-conference

Studying
Thamel, Pete. "The Quad Q&A: Tim Tebow." *The Quad: The New York
Times College Sports Blog. New York Times* online. October 30, 2008.
http://thequad.blogs.nytimes.com/2008/10/30/the-quad-qa-tim-
tebow

Supporting Teammates
Staples, Andy. "Tebow Reprises One-Man Gang Role in Gators' Thumping
of Seminoles." SI.com. November 29, 2008. Updated November 30,
2008. http://sportsillustrated.cnn.com/2008/writers/andy_staples/
11/29/florida.fsu/index.html

Tact

"Tebow Introduced by Jets." NFL.com. Video of Tebow press conference. Transcribed from video. Uploaded on March 26, 2012. http://www.nfl.com/videos/new-york-jets/09000d5d827df421/Tebow-introduced-by-Jets

Tebow Time

"Denver Broncos News Release: Denver Broncos Quotes." November 23, 2011. http://media.denverbroncos.com/images/9008/Transcripts/111123_Tebow.pdf

Tebowing

Velotta, Richard. "Tebow Talks Bible Verses, Ministering, and Tebowing." *Las Vegas Sun* online. March 3, 2012. http://www.lasvegassun.com/news/2012/mar/03/tebow-talks-bible-verses-ministering-tebowing

Temptation

"Tim Tebow on 'Hannity.'" *Fox News* online. Video clip of *Hannity*. Transcribed from video. Uploaded on May 31, 2011. http://video.foxnews.com/v/969875443001/tim-tebow-on-hannity

Tim Tebow Foundation

"Tebow Introduced by Jets." NFL.com. Video of Tebow press conference. Transcribed from video. Uploaded on March 26, 2012. http://www.nfl.com/videos/new-york-jets/09000d5d827df421/Tebow-introduced-by-Jets

Toughness

Carpenter, Les. "Debunking the Myths of Tim Tebow." *Yahoo! Sports.* December 14, 2011. http://sports.yahoo.com/nfl/news?slug=lc-carpenter_tim_tebow_alex_smith draft_broncos_121411

Trash Talking

McCall, Mike. "Trash talk Heats Up Heading into Game against LSU." *The Independent Florida Alligator* online. October 0, 2008. http://www.alligator.org/sports/sports_columns/article_f0bdedfa-be37-5754-8998-aeaf8ccdb063.html

True Satisfaction

"Tim Tebow, Quarterback: Denver Broncos." *Beyond the Ultimate* website. http://www.beyondtheultimate.org/athletes/Tim-Tebow.aspx

Trusting God

Mayne, Kenny. "I Feel Like You Mocked My Question." *ESPN The Magazine.* September 21, 2009. http://insider.espn.go.com/ncf/insider/news/story?id=4455331

Victory

Ramsey, David. "Tebow's Easy Confidence Lifts Broncos." *The Gazette* online. December 15, 2011. http://www.gazette.com/articles/confidence-130238-easy-englewood.html

Visiting Prisoners

Thamel, Pete. "Tim Tebow Visits *The Quad* Q&A." *The Quad: The New York Times College Sports Blog. New York Times* online. September 12, 2007. http://thequad.blogs.nytimes.com/2007/09/12/tim-tebow-visits-the-quad-qa

Visiting Suffering Fans

Reilly, Rick. "I Believe in Tim Tebow." ESPN.com. January 13, 2012. http://espn.go.com/espn/story/_/id/7455943/believing-tim-tebow

What the Future Holds

"Michael Kay: 3/30." ESPNNewYork.com. Audio of radio interview. Transcribed from audio. March 30, 2012. http://espn.go.com/espnradio/newyork/play?id=7757176

ABOUT THE AUTHOR

Jesse Hines is a business writer in southeastern Virginia. He has won first place for local business coverage at the IFPA/SAPA Advertising and Editorial Awards.

Hines, the oldest of six children, was homeschooled, and raised in a Southern Baptist church. Sports have been a significant part of his life since he was a boy, when he played baseball, basketball, or football with his brothers almost every day.